STRONG VOICES

FIFTEEN AMERICAN SPEECHES WORTH KNOWING

STRONG VOICES

FIFTEEN AMERICAN SPEECHES WORTH KNOWING

INTRODUCTIONS BY TONYA BOLDEN

FOREWORD BY COKIE ROBERTS

ILLUSTRATED BY
ERIC VELASQUEZ

HARPER
An Imprint of HarperCollinsPublishers

Strong Voices: Fifteen American Speeches Worth Knowing

Introductions copyright © 2020 by Tonya Bolden

Foreword copyright © 2020 by Cokie Roberts

Illustrations copyright © 2020 by Eric Velasquez

All rights reserved. Printed in the United States of America.

No part of this book may be used or reproduced in any manner whatsoever without written permission except in the case of brief quotations embodied in critical articles and reviews.

For information address HarperCollins Children's Books, a division of HarperCollins Publishers, 195 Broadway, New York, NY 10007.

www.harpercollinschildrens.com

ISBN 978-0-06-257204-2

The artist used oil on watercolor paper to create the illustrations for this book.

Book design by Jeanne Hogle

19 20 21 22 23 PC 10 9 8 7 6 5 4 3 2 1

First Edition

For all the young people who truly
care about America
—T.B.

To all the tirelessly dedicated librarians and
educators who help shape the future
—E.V.

TABLE OF CONTENTS

FOREWORD BY COKIE ROBERTS

At an "awful moment for this country," Patrick Henry dramatically demanded: "Give me liberty or give me death."

> It's not hard for powerful people to speak up for what they believe, but for the powerless it can be downright dangerous.

Those famous words directed at Great Britain have sounded down through the decades since 1775. Henry's timeless demand still echoes in our politics, because it helped define who we are as Americans.

Awful moments provided the contexts for many of these speeches. In 1796, when George Washington issued his farewell address, no one knew if the fledgling United States of America could survive without his leadership.

And in the most awful time of all for America, Abraham Lincoln stood on the battlefield-turned-cemetery at Gettysburg in 1863 and wondered if a nation conceived in liberty with a government "of the people, by the people, and for the people" could long endure.

Though the other speeches here don't share the fame of the Gettysburg Address—it's been translated into some thirty languages—and the orators don't share the power of the president of the United States, we still hear their strong voices.

It's not hard for powerful people to speak up for what they believe, but for the powerless it can be downright dangerous. Thankfully, Red Jacket and Sojourner Truth and Frederick Douglass took that risk—bravely calling on their fellow Americans to extend basic liberties to more and more of the nation.

Calls to action—the only way to overcome the awful moments for the country—abound in these addresses. In 1910 Teddy Roosevelt insisted on an active citizenry in what's come to be called the "man in the arena" speech.

We learn from the people who stepped into that arena, often at great sacrifice. Fanny Lou Hamer described to the delegates at the 1964 Democratic Convention the torture she endured as an African American trying to exercise her right to vote in Mississippi.

Cesar Chavez, the Mexican American founder of the United Farm Workers union, explained to a gathering in 1984 how he was able to bring about better conditions for migrant workers: "We organized!" and then added, "Once social change begins, it cannot be reversed."

But that social change does not begin on its own. Someone must call for it—must raise what is often a lonely voice to insist that all voices be heard and heeded.

Listen then to the people who created this country, kept it from disunion, and brought more of its citizens into the fullness of their rights. With the clarion call "give me liberty" you can hear the sounds of our timeless struggle to fulfill the promise of America, to form a more perfect union.

PUBLISHER'S NOTE

STRONG VOICES IS A COLLEC-TION OF FIFTEEN AMERICAN SPEECHES. SOME YOU'VE HEARD OF—like "Give Me Liberty or Give Me Death," or "The Only Thing We Have to Fear Is Fear Itself," or "I Have a Dream." They represent the "greatest hits"—those that come to mind when you think of famous American speeches. Others you may have never heard of.

Some of the works in this book are complete, and some have been edited, but all have the original words—or at least, the original words as we know them. You see, some weren't written down at the time. And in some cases, they were written down by someone other than the person who gave the speech, so it's complicated. Did the person who wrote it down have their own agenda? Did they alter what was actually said? Some of the speeches are very readable and easy to understand—like Lou Gehrig's "Farewell to Baseball." Others are harder. For each speech, acclaimed writer and history lover Tonya Bolden provides an introduction—telling us what was going on at the time, who the person was, and what it all meant. And along the way, Bolden provides many fascinating insights. Understanding what a speech meant at the time can help unlock what it means for us today. It helps shed light on the ways this nation has changed and the ways that it remains the same.

We hope you'll enjoy this look at fifteen American speeches worth knowing.

PATRICK HENRY

May 29, 1736–June 6, 1799

SPEECH TO SECOND VIRGINIA
CONVENTION, 1775

GIVE ME LIBERTY OR GIVE ME DEATH!

PATRICK HENRY

> If we wish to be free . . . we must fight.

In 1763, with the end of the Seven Years' War between Great Britain and France and their allies, Great Britain controlled more territory. The new land included Canada and what would one day be the United States' Northwest Territory.

But there was a downside.

Debt.

To climb out of the hole, Great Britain imposed more taxes on its thirteen North American colonies. There was the Stamp Act of March 1765, for example. It taxed all manner of printed paper, from newspapers to playing cards. Then came the Townshend Acts, taxing glass and paint, among other imported goods.

People in the thirteen colonies were outraged, especially in Boston, where King George stationed troops in 1768. It was also in Boston that, on March 5, 1770, redcoats, as British soldiers were called, fired into a crowd of rowdy colonists on King Street. The first to fall in this "Boston Massacre" was a seafarer of African descent, Crispus Attucks.

Three years later, in response to a tax on tea and overall British oppression, colonists staged the Boston Tea Party (December 16, 1773). Under cover of night, roughly one hundred men disguised as Mohawk Indians boarded three British ships. They then dumped more than three hundred chests of tea—roughly forty-five tons—into Boston Harbor. Britain retaliated with what Americans called the "Intolerable Acts." For one thing, the port of Boston was closed until all that destroyed tea was paid for—tea worth about $1 million in today's dollars. Even more infuriating, Great Britain put Massachusetts under military rule. Colonists' anger over this—and over so much taxation without representation in Parliament—burned even more fiercely.

What to do?

From September 5 through October 26, 1774, white male land-owning delegates from twelve colonies (Georgia abstained) met in Philadelphia. These men decided to launch a boycott of British goods and to petition King George to repeal the Intolerable Acts. Patrick Henry of Virginia was one of the fifty-six delegates at this First Continental Congress.

Several months later, roughly one hundred white men met in Richmond, Virginia's

St. John's Church for a weeklong Second Virginia Convention. (The first was held after passage of the Intolerable Acts.)

These Virginians seeking liberty from British tyranny included the wealthy slaveholders Thomas Jefferson and George Washington. Patrick Henry, a slaveholder, too, was also there. This failed grocer, failed farmer, failed shopkeeper, then bartender and fiddler, had become a successful lawyer and a member of Virginia's House of Burgesses (general assembly).

On Thursday, March 23, 1775, day four of the Second Virginia Convention, Patrick Henry urged his colony to prepare to protect itself from an increasingly menacing Great Britain by raising a militia. Most delegates recoiled at the idea. That could provoke a wholesale British invasion!

When debate ceased, Patrick Henry rose from his seat with "an unearthly fire burning in his eye," remembered one witness. The "tendons of his neck stood out white and rigid like whipcords." Henry argued that there was absolutely, positively no hope for reconciliation with Great Britain. In closing, to the spellbound crowd, he declared—

"Give me liberty . . ."

His left arm was at his side.

In his right hand he held an ivory letter opener aimed at his chest.

". . . or give me death!"

But wait—is that how it really went down?

Historians now think that this firebrand made up his riveting speech as he went along. And remember, there were no audio or video recording devices back then.

Patrick Henry's speech did not appear in print until forty years after he delivered it, long after his death.

Regardless of what Henry actually said, there is no doubt that his words made a difference. After he spoke, a resolution to raise a Virginia militia passed 65–60.

"Liberty or Death" became a Patriot battle cry during the American Revolution, which began with the Battles of Lexington and Concord on April 19, 1775, twenty-seven days after Patrick Henry's rousing speech.

THIS IS NO TIME FOR CEREMONY. THE QUESTION BEFORE THE HOUSE IS ONE OF AWFUL MOMENT TO THIS COUNTRY. FOR MY OWN PART, I CONSIDER IT AS NOTHING LESS THAN A QUESTION OF FREEDOM OR SLAVERY; AND IN PROPORTION TO THE MAGNITUDE OF THE SUBJECT OUGHT TO BE THE FREEDOM OF THE DEBATE. IT IS ONLY IN THIS WAY THAT WE CAN HOPE TO ARRIVE AT TRUTH, AND FULFILL THE GREAT RESPONSIBILITY WHICH WE HOLD TO GOD AND OUR COUNTRY. . . .

For my part, whatever anguish of spirit it may cost, I am willing to know the whole truth; to know the worst, and to provide for it.

I have but one lamp by which my feet are guided, and that is the lamp of experience. I know of no way of judging of the future but by the past. And judging by the past, I wish to know what there has been in the conduct of the British ministry for the last ten years to justify those hopes with which gentlemen have been pleased to solace themselves and the House. Is it that insidious smile with which our petition has been lately received? Trust it not, sir; it will prove a snare to your feet. Suffer not yourselves to be betrayed with a kiss. Ask yourselves how this gracious reception of our petition comports with these warlike preparations which cover our waters and darken our land. Are fleets and armies necessary to a work of love and recon-

ciliation? Have we shown ourselves so unwilling to be reconciled that force must be called in to win back our love? Let us not deceive ourselves, sir. These are the implements of war and subjugation; the last arguments to which kings resort.

I ask gentlemen, sir, what means this martial array, if its purpose be not to force us to submission? Can gentlemen assign any other possible motive for it? Has Great Britain any enemy, in this quarter of the world, to call for all this accumulation of navies and armies? No, sir, she has none. They are meant for us; they can be meant for no other. . . .

Sir, we have done everything that could be done to avert the storm which is now coming on. We have petitioned; we have remonstrated; we have supplicated; we have prostrated ourselves before the throne, and have implored its interposition to arrest the tyrannical hands of the ministry and Parliament. Our petitions

have been slighted; our remonstrances have produced additional violence and insult; our supplications have been disregarded; and we have been spurned, with contempt, from the foot of the throne. In vain, after these things, may we indulge the fond hope of peace and reconciliation. There is no longer any room for hope. If we wish to be free . . . we must fight! I repeat it, sir, we must fight! An appeal to arms and to the God of hosts is all that is left us!

They tell us, sir, that we are weak; unable to cope with so formidable an adversary. But when shall we be stronger? Will it be the next week, or the next year? Will it be when we are totally disarmed, and when a British guard shall be stationed in every house? . . .

Sir, we are not weak if we make a proper use of those means which the God of nature hath placed in our power. . . .

There is no retreat but in submission and slavery! Our chains are forged! Their clanking may be heard on the plains of Boston! The war is inevitable—and let it come! I repeat it, sir, let it come.

It is in vain, sir, to extenuate the matter. Gentlemen may cry, Peace, Peace—but there is no peace. The war is actually begun! The next gale that sweeps from the north will bring to our ears the clash of resounding arms! Our brethren are already in the field! Why stand we here idle? What is it that gentlemen wish? What would they have? Is life so dear, or peace so sweet, as to be purchased at the price of chains and slavery? Forbid it, Almighty God! I know not what course others may take; but as for me, give me liberty or give me death!

GEORGE WASHINGTON

FEBRUARY 22, 1732–DECEMBER 14, 1799

LETTER TO THE AMERICAN PEOPLE
AT THE END OF WASHINGTON'S
SECOND PRESIDENTIAL TERM, 1796

FAREWELL ADDRESS

GEORGE WASHINGTON

[Political parties] are likely . . . to become potent engines, by which cunning, ambitious, and unprincipled men will be enabled to subvert the power of the people.

On February 23, 1994, Illinois's Carol Moseley-Braun, the first black female US senator, had the honor of taking to the Senate floor to do something no one like her had ever done.

Moseley-Braun was the first person of African descent to read aloud to colleagues in the Capitol the farewell address of President George Washington. His roughly seven-thousand-word text first appeared in the September 19, 1796, issue of the *American Daily Advertiser*, a newspaper published in Philadelphia, the nation's capital at the time.

In 1796, George Washington was sixty-four and not in the best of health. He yearned to return to the quiet life on his plantation in Mount Vernon, Virginia.

Today a president can serve only two terms, but back then there were no term limits. Washington, who had served as the commander in chief of the Continental Army during the Revolution, then two terms as the nation's first president, was very popular. Many Americans wanted him to serve a third term as president. But, no, Washington finally made up his mind. No third term. Thus, his farewell address, which he never read in public.

In this address, Washington offered his fellow Americans some very sage advice. He encouraged them to steer clear of foreign entanglements (or permanent pacts with other countries). He cautioned against racking up massive debt. Above all, preserve the Union!

To that end, Washington urged the nation to just say no to vicious political and sectional partisanship; that is, putting one's political party or region above the good of the nation. The president also implored America to maintain the checks and balances provided by the US Constitution, the supreme law of the land, which created the three branches of the government—the legislative (the US Congress), the executive (the presidency),

and the judicial (the US Supreme Court)—allowing one branch to challenge another so that no one branch would have absolute power, absolute rule.

Washington's Farewell Address came twenty years after the Declaration of Independence and eight years after the ratification of the US Constitution. The young nation was fragile. Many worried that it would not endure. There was talk of states going their separate ways.

Over the years American politicians and ordinary citizens have turned to George Washington's Farewell Address in times of crises, especially during days of hyperpartisanship. They turn to it as a morale booster, as a call for national unity.

The first reading of Washington's Farewell Address inside the Capitol occurred during the Civil War (1861–1865), in which eleven Southern slaveholding states that had broken away from the United States fought to be an independent nation. It was a time when Americans who remained loyal to the Union could definitely use some morale boosting, a reinvigoration of their faith in the Union.

On February 22, 1862, the 130th anniversary of George Washington's birth, Secretary of the Senate John W. Forney read this Farewell Address to a joint session of Congress. Its reading on the day of Washington's birthday observance still continues to this day in the Senate.

In January 2017, at a time of a very divided America, the nation's 44th president, Barack Hussein Obama, made reference to Washington's Farewell Address in his own farewell address after two terms in office. For one thing, Obama reminded the nation that Washington had urged Americans to guard against "'every attempt to alienate [or isolate] any portion of our country from the rest or to enfeeble [or weaken] the sacred ties' that make us one."

THE PERIOD FOR A NEW ELECTION OF A CITIZEN TO ADMINISTER THE EXECUTIVE GOVERNMENT OF THE UNITED STATES BEING NOT FAR DISTANT, AND THE TIME ACTUALLY ARRIVED WHEN YOUR THOUGHTS MUST BE EMPLOYED IN DESIGNATING THE PERSON WHO IS TO BE CLOTHED WITH THAT IMPORTANT TRUST, IT APPEARS TO ME PROPER, ESPECIALLY AS IT MAY CONDUCE TO A MORE DISTINCT EXPRESSION OF THE PUBLIC VOICE, THAT I SHOULD NOW APPRISE YOU OF THE RESOLUTION I HAVE FORMED,

to decline being considered among the number of those out of whom a choice is to be made. . . . Here, perhaps, I ought to stop. But a solicitude for your welfare, which cannot end but with my life, and the apprehension of danger, natural to that solicitude, urge me, on an occasion like the present, to offer to your solemn contemplation, and to recommend to your frequent review, some sentiments which are the result of much reflection. . . .

The unity of government which constitutes you one people is also now dear to you. It is justly so, for it is a main pillar in the edifice of your real independence, the support of your tranquility at home, your peace abroad; of your safety; of your prosperity; of that very liberty which you so highly prize. But as it is easy to foresee that, from different causes and from different quarters, much pains

will be taken, . . . it is of infinite moment that you should properly estimate the immense value of your national union to your collective and individual happiness; that you should cherish a cordial, habitual, and immovable attachment to it; accustoming yourselves to think and speak of it as of the palladium [or source of protection] of your political safety and prosperity; watching for its preservation with jealous anxiety; discountenancing whatever may suggest even a suspicion that it can in any event be abandoned; and indignantly frowning upon the first dawning of every attempt to alienate any portion of our country from the rest, or to enfeeble the sacred ties which now link together the various parts. . . .

To the [effectiveness] and permanency of your Union, a government for the whole is indispensable. No alliance, however strict, between the parts can be an adequate substitute; they must inevitably experience the infractions and interruptions which all alliances in all times have experienced. . . . This government, the offspring of our own choice, uninfluenced and unawed, adopted upon full investigation and mature deliberation, completely free in its principles, in the distribution of its powers, uniting security with energy, and containing within itself a provision for its own amendment, has a just claim to your confidence and your support. Respect for its authority, compliance with its laws, acquiescence in its measures, are duties enjoined by the fundamental maxims of true liberty. The basis of our political systems is the right of the people to make and to alter their constitutions of government. But the Constitution which at any time exists, till changed by an explicit and authentic act of the whole people, is sacredly obligatory upon all. The very idea of the power and the right of the people to establish government presupposes the duty of every individual to obey the established government.

All obstructions to the execution of the laws, all combinations and associations, under whatever plausible character, with the real design to direct, control, counteract, or awe the regular deliberation and action of the constituted authorities, are destructive of this fundamental principle, and of fatal tendency. . . .

However combinations or associations of the above description may now and then answer popular ends, [political parties] are likely . . . to become potent engines, by which cunning, ambitious, and unprincipled men will be enabled to subvert the power of the people and to usurp for themselves the reins of government, destroying afterwards the very engines which have lifted them to unjust dominion.

Towards the preservation of your government, and the permanency of your present happy state, it is requisite, not only that you steadily discountenance irregular oppositions to its acknowledged authority, but also that you resist with care the spirit of innovation upon its principles. . . . In all the changes to which you may be invited, remember that time and habit are at least as necessary to fix the true character of governments as of other human institutions; that experience is the surest standard by which to test the real tendency of the existing constitution of a country; that facility in changes, upon the credit of mere hypothesis and opinion, exposes to perpetual change, from the endless variety of hypothesis and opinion; and remember, especially, that for the efficient management of your common interests, in a country so extensive as ours, a government of as much vigor as is consistent with the perfect security of liberty is indispensable. Liberty itself will find in such a government, with powers properly distributed and adjusted, its surest guardian. . . .

It is important, likewise, that the habits of thinking in a free country should inspire caution in those entrusted with its administration, to confine themselves within their respective constitutional spheres, avoiding in the exercise of the powers of one department to encroach upon another. The spirit of encroachment tends to consolidate the powers of all the departments in one, and thus to create, whatever the form of government, a real despotism. A just estimate of that love of power, and proneness to abuse it, which predominates in the human heart, is sufficient to satisfy us of the truth of this position. The necessity of reciprocal checks in the exercise of political power, by dividing and distributing it into different depositaries, and constituting each the guardian of the public weal [well-being] against invasions by the others, has been evinced by experiments ancient and modern; some of them in our country and under our own eyes. To preserve them must be as necessary as to institute them. If, in the opinion of the people, the distribution or modification of the constitutional powers be in any particular wrong, let it be corrected by an amendment in the way which the Constitution designates. But let there be no change by usurpation; for though this, in one instance, may be the instrument of good, it is the customary weapon by which free governments are destroyed. . . .

Observe good faith and justice towards all nations; cultivate peace and harmony with all. . . . Antipathy in one nation against another disposes each more readily to offer insult and injury, to lay hold of slight causes of umbrage, and to be haughty and intractable, when accidental or trifling occasions of dispute occur. . . . So likewise, a passionate attachment of one nation for another produces a variety of evils. . . . Against the insidious wiles of foreign influence (I conjure you to believe me, fellow-citizens) the jealousy of a free people ought to be constantly awake, since history and experience prove that foreign influence is one of the most baneful foes of republican government. . . . In offering to you, my countrymen, these counsels of an old and affectionate friend, I dare not hope they will make the strong and lasting impression I could wish; that they will control the usual current of the passions, or prevent our nation from running the course which has hitherto marked the destiny of nations. . . .

Though, in reviewing the incidents of my administration, I am unconscious of intentional error, I am nevertheless too sensible of my defects not to think it probable that I may have committed many errors. Whatever they may be, I fervently beseech the Almighty to avert or mitigate the evils to which they may tend. I shall also carry with me the hope that my country will never cease to view them with indulgence; and that, after forty five years of my life dedicated to its service with an upright zeal, the faults of incompetent abilities will be consigned to oblivion, as myself must soon be to the mansions of rest.

Relying on its kindness in this as in other things, and actuated by that fervent love towards it, which is so natural to a man who views in it the native soil of himself and his progenitors for several generations, I anticipate with pleasing expectation that retreat in which I promise myself to realize, without alloy, the sweet enjoyment of partaking, in the midst of my fellow-citizens, the benign influence of good laws under a free government, the ever-favorite object of my heart, and the happy reward, as I trust, of our mutual cares, labors, and dangers.

RED JACKET

C. 1758–January 20, 1830

REPLY TO REV. JACOB CRAM, 1805 (?)

WE NEVER QUARREL ABOUT RELIGION

Brother,
we do not wish to
destroy your religion, or
take it from you;
we only want
to enjoy our own.

RED JACKET

This member of the Seneca's Wolf Clan was called Red Jacket by whites and Native Americans alike because there was a time when he reveled in wearing a red coat British officers gave him for his service as a messenger during the American Revolution (1775–1783). The pride Red Jacket took in that piece of clothing was nothing like the pride he took in his heritage, his peoples' customs and traditions.

Red Jacket's given name was Otetiani ("always ready"). This resident of western New York State was later renamed Sagoyewatha (Shay-gó-ye-wátha or Say-go-ye-watah). The name's translations include "disturber of dreams" and "he keeps us awake."

This renowned Native American orator most definitely sought to keep his people awake and aware when a Boston missionary named Reverend Jacob Cram urged the Seneca to abandon their belief system and embrace Christianity.

"There is but one religion, and but one way to serve God," said Jacob Cram, "and if you do not embrace the right way, you cannot be happy hereafter. You have never worshipped the Great Spirit in the manner acceptable to him; but have, all your lives, been in great errors and darkness."

Speaking through an interpreter, Chief Red Jacket respectfully disagreed. With grace and pinches of wit, Red Jacket reminded Reverend Cram of how white people had so often deceived and run roughshod over Native Americans. He asked the arrogant missionary to explain why white people quarreled over religion among themselves if in fact there was but one way to serve the Great Spirit.

Red Jacket delivered this, his most famous speech, in late 1805 or early 1806. It first appeared in print in April 1809, in the magazine *Monthly Anthology, and Boston Review.*

After Cram condemned the Seneca's religion, Red Jacket redoubled his efforts to get his people to remain true to their traditional beliefs. His campaign climaxed with the three-year ban (1821–1824) on Christian missionaries living on Seneca land. The disturber of dreams was later deeply grieved when members of his own family converted to Christianity.

BROTHER, THIS COUNCIL FIRE WAS KINDLED BY YOU; IT WAS AT YOUR REQUEST THAT WE CAME TOGETHER AT THIS TIME; WE HAVE LISTENED WITH ATTENTION TO WHAT YOU HAVE SAID. YOU REQUESTED US TO SPEAK OUR MINDS FREELY; THIS GIVES US GREAT JOY, FOR WE NOW CONSIDER THAT WE STAND UPRIGHT BEFORE YOU, AND CAN SPEAK WHAT WE THINK; ALL HAVE HEARD YOUR VOICE, AND ALL SPEAK TO YOU AS ONE MAN; OUR MINDS ARE AGREED. . . .

Brother, listen to what we say. There was a time when our forefathers owned this great island. Their seats extended from the rising to the setting sun. The Great Spirit had made it for the use of Indians. He had created the buffalo, the deer, and other animals for food. He made the bear and the beaver, and their skins served us for clothing. He had scattered them over the country, and taught us how to take them. He had caused the earth to produce corn for bread. All this he had done for his red children because he loved them. If we had any disputes about hunting grounds, they were generally settled without the shedding of much blood. But an evil day came upon us; your forefathers crossed the great waters, and landed [here]. Their numbers were small; they found friends, and not enemies; they told us they had fled from their own country for fear of wicked men, and come here to enjoy their religion. They asked for a small seat; we took pity on them, granted their request, and they sat down amongst us; we gave them corn and meat; they gave us poison in return. . . . At length, their numbers had greatly increased; they wanted more land; they wanted our country. Our eyes were opened, and our minds became uneasy. Wars took place; Indians were hired to fight against Indians, and many of our people were destroyed. They also brought strong liquor among us; it was strong and powerful, and has slain thousands.

Brother, our seats were once large, and yours were very small; you have now become a great people, and we have scarcely a place left to spread our blankets; you have got our country, but are not satisfied; you want to force your religion upon us.

Brother, continue to listen. You say you are sent to instruct us how to worship the Great Spirit agreeably to his mind, and if we do not take hold of the religion which you white people teach, we shall be unhappy hereafter. You say that you are right, and we are lost; how do we know this to be true? We understand that your religion is written in a book; if it was intended for us as well as you, why has not the Great Spirit given it to us, and not only to us, but why did he not give to our forefathers the knowledge of that book, with the means of understanding it rightly? We only know what you tell us about it. How shall we know when to believe, being so often deceived by the white people?

Brother, you say there is but one way to worship and serve the Great Spirit; if there is but one religion, why do you white people differ so much about it? Why not all agree, as you can all read the book?

Brother, we do not understand these things. We are told that your religion was given to your forefathers, and has been handed down from father to son. We also have a religion which was given to our forefathers, and has been handed down to us their children. We worship that way. It teacheth us to be thankful for all the favors we receive; to love each other, and to be united. We never quarrel about religion. . . .

Brother, we do not wish to destroy your religion, or take it from you; we only want to enjoy our own.

FREDERICK DOUGLASS

c. February 14, 1818–February 20, 1895

SPEECH AT AN EVENT COMMEMORATING
THE SIGNING OF THE DECLARATION
OF INDEPENDENCE, JULY 5, 1852

WHAT TO THE SLAVE IS THE FOURTH OF JULY?

FREDERICK DOUGLASS

A ctivist and entrepreneur Frederick Douglass, possessed of a voice as rich and powerful as his mind, was born into slavery on Maryland's eastern shore as Frederick Augustus Washington Bailey.

Inquisitive since childhood and self-taught, Frederick Douglass pulled off his great escape at age twenty, on September 3, 1838, settling in New Bedford, Massachusetts. There he became an abolitionist, someone calling for the immediate end of slavery.

Because of his eloquence and majestic presence, Douglass, who was over six feet tall, quickly became one of the most sought-after abolitionist lecturers—doubly so after the publication of his first autobiography, *Narrative of the Life of Frederick Douglass* (1845). Two years later, the first edition of his first newspaper, the *North Star*, rolled off the presses. By then Douglass was living in Rochester, New York.

It was there that on July 5, 1852, Frederick Douglass delivered one of his best-known speeches. More than five hundred people packed into the city's Corinthian Hall to hear him. The price of the ticket was twelve cents.

> This Fourth [of] July is yours, not mine. You may rejoice, I must mourn. . . .

Douglass's speech was an impassioned plea for justice, for an end to what he called the "twin-monsters of darkness"—racism and slavery. He urged the nation to live up to its ideals—to its creed that "all men are created equal, that they are endowed by their Creator with certain unalienable Rights, that among these are Life, Liberty and the Pursuit of Happiness," as stated in the Declaration of Independence, adopted by the nation's founders seventy-six years earlier on July 4, 1776.

In searing, soaring prose, Douglass took his beloved country to task for its hypocrisy. Its treatment of black people was not in keeping with its creed.

Though Douglass spoke mostly about the horrors some 3.2 million enslaved men and women, girls and boys suffered, he was just as concerned about the plight of the nation's half-million free black women and men, girls and boys, who constantly faced discrimination.

Until racial wrongs were righted, Frederick Douglass was not about to celebrate Independence Day. He urged others to do likewise.

"Fellow-citizens, pardon me, allow me to ask, why am I called upon to speak here today?" Douglass inquired at one point. "What have I, or those I represent, to do with your national independence?"

That was merely a rhetorical flourish, for Douglass knew well that he was speaking to like-minded people. The crowd was composed of abolitionists, hungry for his oratory, hungry for his inspiration. And Douglass had come prepared. He had brought along copies of his speech in the form of a thirty-nine-page pamphlet. Seven hundred sold immediately.

Frederick Douglass's own title for this speech was "The Meaning of July Fourth for the Negro." The title it's known by today was inspired by perhaps the most poignant passage. That sentence is "What, to the American slave, is your 4th of July?"

THE FACT IS, LADIES AND GENTLEMEN, THE DISTANCE BETWEEN THIS PLATFORM ANDTHE SLAVE PLANTATION, FROM WHICH I ESCAPED, IS CONSIDERABLE—AND THE DIFFICULTIES TO BE OVERCOME IN GETTING FROM THE LATTER TO THE FORMER, ARE BY NO MEANS SLIGHT. THAT I AM HERE TO-DAY IS, TO ME, A MATTER OF ASTONISHMENT AS WELL AS OF GRATITUDE. . . .

The 4th of July is the first great fact in your nation's history—the very ring-bolt in the chain of your yet undeveloped destiny.

Pride and patriotism, not less than gratitude, prompt you to celebrate and to hold it in perpetual remembrance. . . .

Fellow Citizens, I am not wanting in respect for the fathers of this republic. The signers of the Declaration of Independence were brave men. They were great men too—great enough to give fame to a great age. It does not often happen to a nation to raise, at one time, such a number of truly great men. The point from which I am compelled to view them is not, certainly, the most favorable; and yet I cannot contemplate their great deeds with less than admiration. They were statesmen, patriots and heroes, and for the good they did, and the principles they contended for, I will unite with you to honor their memory. . . .

Friends and citizens, I need not enter further into the causes which led to this anniversary. Many of you understand them better than I do. You could instruct me in regard to them. That is a branch of knowledge in which you feel, perhaps, a much deeper interest than your speaker. The causes which led to the separation of the colonies from the British crown have never lacked for a tongue. They have all been taught in your common schools, narrated at your firesides, unfolded from your pulpits, and thundered from your legislative halls, and are as familiar to you as household words. They form the staple of your national poetry and eloquence.

I remember, also, that, as a people, Americans are remarkably familiar with all facts which make in their own favor. This is esteemed by some as a national trait—perhaps a national weakness. It is a fact, that whatever makes for the wealth or for the reputation of Americans, and can be had cheap! will be found by Americans. I shall not be charged with slandering Americans, if I say I think the American side of any question may be safely left in American hands. . . .

Washington could not die till he had broken the chains of his slaves. Yet his monument is built up by the price of human blood, and the traders in the bodies and souls of men shout—"We have Washington to *our father.*"—Alas! that it should be so; yet so it is.

The evil that men do lives after them. The good is oft interred with their bones.

Fellow-citizens, pardon me, allow me to ask, why am I called upon to speak here to-day? What have I, or those I represent, to do with your national independence? Are the great principles of political freedom and of natural justice, embodied in that Declaration of Independence, extended to us? and am I, therefore, called upon to bring our humble offering to the national altar, and to confess the benefits and express devout gratitude for the blessings resulting from your independence to us?

Would to God, both for your sakes and ours, that an affirmative answer could be truthfully returned to these questions! Then would my task be light, and my burden easy and delightful. . . .

But, such is not the state of the case. I say it with a sad sense of the disparity between us. I am not included within the pale of this glorious anniversary! Your high independence only reveals the immeasurable distance between us. The blessings in which you, this day, rejoice, are not enjoyed in common.—The rich inheritance of justice, liberty, prosperity and independence, bequeathed by your fathers, is shared by you, not by me. The sunlight that brought life and healing to you, has brought stripes and death to me. This Fourth [of] July is *yours*, not *mine*. *You* may rejoice, *I* must mourn. . . .

Fellow-citizens; above your national, tumultuous joy, I hear the mournful wail of millions! whose chains, heavy and grievous yesterday, are, to-day, rendered more intolerable by the jubilee shouts that reach them. If I do forget, if I do not faithfully remember those bleeding children of sorrow this day, "may my right hand forget her cunning, and may my tongue cleave to the roof of my mouth!" To forget them, to pass lightly over their wrongs, and to chime in with the popular theme, would be treason most scandalous and shocking, and would make me a reproach before God and the world. My subject, then fellow-citizens, is AMERICAN SLAVERY. I shall see, this day, and its popular characteristics, from the slave's point of view. . .

America is false to the past, false to the present, and solemnly binds herself to be false to the future. Standing with God and the crushed and bleeding slave on this occasion, I will, in the name of humanity which is outraged, in the name of liberty which is fettered, in the name of the constitution and the Bible, which are disregarded and trampled upon, dare to call in question and to denounce, with all the emphasis I can command, everything that serves to perpetuate slavery—the great sin and shame of America! . . .

But I fancy I hear some one of my audience say, it is just in this circumstance that you and your brother abolitionists fail to make a favorable impression on the public mind. Would you argue more, and denounce less, would you persuade more, and rebuke less, your cause would be much more likely to succeed. But, I submit, where all is plain there is nothing to be argued. . . . Must I undertake to prove that the slave is a man? That point is conceded already. Nobody doubts it. The slaveholders themselves acknowledge it in the enactment of laws for their government. They acknowledge it when they punish disobedience on the part of the slave. There

are seventy-two crimes in the State of Virginia, which, if committed by a black man, (no matter how ignorant he be), subject him to the punishment of death; while only two of the same crimes will subject a white man to the like punishment. What is this but the acknowledgement that the slave is a moral, intellectual and responsible being? . . .

For the present, it is enough to affirm the equal manhood of the Negro race. Is it not astonishing that, while we are ploughing, planting and reaping, using all kinds of mechanical tools, erecting houses, constructing bridges, building ships, working in metals of brass, iron, copper, silver and gold; that, while we are reading, writing and cyphering, acting as clerks, merchants and secretaries, having among us lawyers, doctors, ministers, poets, authors, editors, orators and teachers; that, while we are engaged in all manner of enterprises common to other men, digging gold in California, capturing the whale in the Pacific, feeding sheep and cattle on the hill-side, living, moving, acting, thinking, planning, living in families as husbands, wives and children, and, above all, confessing and worshipping the Christian's God, and looking hopefully for life and immortality beyond the grave, we are called upon to prove that we are men!

Would you have me argue that man is entitled to liberty? that he is the rightful owner of his own body? You have already declared it. Must I argue the wrongfulness of slavery? . . . There is not a man beneath the canopy of heaven, that does not know that slavery is wrong *for him*. . . .

What, to the American slave, is your 4th of July? I answer: a day that reveals to him, more than all other days in the year, the gross injustice and cruelty to which he is the constant victim. To him, your celebration is a sham; your boasted liberty, an unholy license; your national greatness, swelling vanity; your sounds of rejoicing are empty and heartless; your denunciations of tyrants, brass fronted impudence; your shouts of liberty and equality, hollow mockery; your prayers and hymns, your sermons and thanksgivings, with all your religious parade, and solemnity, are, to him, mere bombast, fraud, deception, impiety, and hypocrisy—a thin veil to cover up crimes which would disgrace a nation of savages. There is not a nation on the earth guilty of practices, more shocking and bloody, than are the people of these United States, at this very hour.

SOJOURNER TRUTH

C. 1797–NOVEMBER 26, 1883

SPEECH AT THE WOMEN'S RIGHTS
CONVENTION IN AKRON, OHIO, 1851

I AM A WOMAN'S RIGHTS

SOJOURNER TRUTH

> Why children, if you have woman's rights, give it to her and you will feel better.

A "strange compound of wit and wisdom, of wild enthusiasm and flint-like common sense." That's how Frederick Douglass described the woman born into slavery as Isabella Bomefree (also spelled Baumfree) in Ulster County, New York, a woman who endured ceaseless toil and abuse for years, a woman who walked away from slavery in 1826, a year before slavery ended in New York State.

And this woman later testified that God had given her a new name.

Sojourner—because she was to move about, staying only briefly in any one place.

Truth—because that was what she was to proclaim as she preached the word of God.

This occurred in the spring of 1843 in New York City, where she was a domestic worker. Answering the call to preach, Sojourner Truth gathered up her meager belongings in a pillowcase, a basket of provisions, and two York shillings, then took to the road.

As an itinerant preacher, Sojourner Truth captivated audiences in camp meetings and at other venues in the Northeast. "A woman of remarkable intelligence despite her illiteracy, Truth had a great presence," writes scholar Nell Irvin Painter. "She was tall, some 5 feet 11 inches, of spare but solid frame. Her voice was low, so low that listeners sometimes termed it masculine, and her singing voice was beautifully powerful."

Just as Truth urged people to serve God and live holy, she also exhorted them to do right by black people and women. Her most notable call for gender equality—for women to have true liberty—was delivered on May 29, 1851, during a women's rights convention in Akron, Ohio. In just a few words, words honeyed with humor and bearing Biblical references, the towering figure in her mid-fifties addressed the fears that many white men had of women's rights, just as they did of black freedom and civil rights. Such men saw equality of opportunity for all as a grave threat to their power. Such men believed that America was a "white man's country."

When Sojourner Truth spoke at the convention in Akron, many American colleges and universities would not admit women. Women were basically told that their "place" was in the home—and definitely not in the political sphere. You see, women did not have the right to vote.

Even before the Akron convention, women had begun to campaign for their rights, including the right to vote. Many of the leaders of the movement were well-off white women such as writer and abolitionist Frances Dana Gage, who organized the convention in Akron.

Twelve years later, in April 1863, the *New York Independent* published Sojourner Truth's speech, which Gage had provided. For years people believed that what the *Independent* printed—a piece punctuated with the refrain "Ain't I a woman"—was gospel. Hmm.

"Well, chillen, whar dar's so much racket dar must be som'ting out o'kilter," began the Gage version. And it continued on in exaggerated Southern dialect.

That's odd.

Truth was a Northerner. If anything, she would have had a Dutch accent, as that was her first language, the language of her first owners. Gage's version of the speech even had Sojourner Truth dropping the N-word. Gage also reported that Truth faced hissing and booing in Akron.

In contrast, the white man Marius R. Robinson, the convention's recording secretary and someone who knew Truth well, told a different story.

"It is impossible to transfer it to paper, or convey any adequate idea of the effect it produced upon the audience," wrote Robinson. "Those only can appreciate it who saw her powerful form, her whole-souled, earnest gesture, and listened to her strong and truthful tones."

With these words, Robinson introduced a version of Truth's speech that appeared a month after the convention in his newspaper, the *Anti-Slavery Bugle*, published in Salem, Ohio, about fifty miles southeast of Akron as the crow flies. The Robinson version, devoid of dialect and vulgarity, is reprinted here.

You need not be afraid to give us our rights for fear we will take too much . . .

MAY I SAY A FEW WORDS? RECEIVING AN AFFIRMATIVE ANSWER, SHE PROCEEDED; I WANT TO SAY A FEW WORDS ABOUT THIS MATTER. I AM A WOMAN'S RIGHTS. I HAVE AS MUCH MUSCLE AS ANY MAN, AND CAN DO AS MUCH WORK AS ANY MAN. I HAVE PLOWED AND REAPED AND HUSKED AND CHOPPED AND MOWED, AND CAN ANY MAN DO MORE THAN THAT?

I have heard much about the sexes being equal; I can carry as much as any man, and can eat as much too, if I can get it. I am strong as any man that is now. As for intellect, all I can say is, if woman have a pint and man a quart—why can't she have her little pint full? You need not be afraid to give us our rights for fear we will take too much—for we won't take more than our pint'll hold.

The poor men seem to be all in confusion and don't know what to do. Why children, if you have woman's rights give it to her and you will feel better. You will have your own rights, and they won't be so much trouble.

I can't read, but I can hear. I have heard the Bible and have learned that Eve caused man to sin. Well if woman upset the world, do give her a chance to set it right side up again.

The lady has spoken about Jesus, how he never spurned woman from him, and she was right. When Lazarus died, Mary and Martha came to him with faith and love and besought him to raise their brother. And Jesus wept—and Lazarus came forth. And how came Jesus into the world? Through God who created him and woman who bore him. Man, where is your part?

But the women are coming up blessed be God and a few of the men are coming up with them. But man is in a tight place, the poor slave is on him, woman is coming on him, and he is surely between a hawk and a buzzard.

ABRAHAM LINCOLN

FEBRUARY 12, 1809–APRIL 15, 1865

SPEECH AT THE DEDICATION OF THE SOLDIERS' NATIONAL CEMETERY, GETTYSBURG, PENNSYLVANIA, 1863

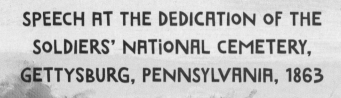

GETTYSBURG ADDRESS

ABRAHAM LINCOLN

> Now we are engaged in a great civil war . . . testing whether that nation, or any nation so conceived and so dedicated . . . can long endure.

"A GLORIOUS VICTORY!" read a headline in the *Boston Daily Advertiser* on July 6, 1863.

The newspaper was trumpeting the Union's victory in the bloodiest battle of the Civil War: the July 1–July 3, 1863, fight in Gettysburg, Pennsylvania. On the Fourth of July, beneath a pouting, raining sky, Confederate troops, under the command of General Robert E. Lee, were in retreat, never again to attempt an invasion of the North.

The Battle of Gettysburg claimed the lives of more than three thousand Union soldiers and nearly four thousand Confederate ones. Roughly forty-three thousand Union and Confederate men and boys were left wounded, missing, or captured.

In the aftermath of the battle, Pennsylvania's governor, Andrew Curtin, asked Gettysburg resident David Wills, an attorney, to oversee the burial of the Union's fallen. Wills, however, became obsessed with doing something more. He proposed a national cemetery on the battlefield, a proposal to which Governor Curtin agreed. The dedication day was eventually set for November 19, 1863.

The Union's president, Abraham Lincoln, was not at the top of the list when invitations went out to VIPs. Some of the men working on the program feared that Lincoln's presence might make the event too political. But how could they not invite the president?

Finally, on November 2, 1863, Wills sent Lincoln an invitation. He asked the president to deliver "a few appropriate remarks."

At first Lincoln didn't think that he could attend the event. He was in the midst of managing a fractured nation, after all. Too, in December he had to deliver the Annual Message to Congress (today's State of the Union). It was a speech he had yet to get cracking on. What's more, his ten-year-old son, Tad, was quite ill.

Not until Monday, November 16—three days before the event—did the public learn that, yes, the president would attend the

dedication of the Soldiers' National Cemetery in Gettysburg.

With his two private secretaries, several cabinet members, and other Washingtonians, the president boarded a morning train on November 18, "sallow, sunken-eyed, thin, careworn and very quiet," remembered one companion. Once in Gettysburg, Lincoln lodged in David Wills's home, in a second-floor room. The next morning, he viewed the battlefield before heading to the dedication service.

"Standing beneath this serene sky, overlooking these broad fields," began the keynote address of Edward Everett, one of the finest orators of the day. Roughly thirteen thousand words later, Everett closed with this: "in the glorious annals of our common country there will be no brighter page than that which relates THE BATTLES OF GETTYSBURG."

Two hours had elapsed.

President Lincoln was no stranger to long speeches—not to hearing them, not to giving them. But on this day, he heeded Wills's request for just "a few appropriate remarks."

The six-foot-four, lanky Abraham Lincoln, wearing a new black suit, a speaker not prone to gesticulations and mighty movement,

addressed the crowd in simple terms. Chiefly, he expressed his earnest hope that the fallen did not die in vain and that the nation would have "a new birth of freedom."

Lincoln's speech, fewer than three hundred words, was delivered in under three minutes.

For years people believed that Lincoln dashed off the Gettysburg Address on an envelope during his train ride to the town. In fact, he began working on the speech days before he boarded that train. He revised it during the journey. He revised it again in Gettysburg, after he surveyed the battlefield the morning of the dedication service. Lincoln's writing and rewriting resulted in a speech that met with tremendous applause.

The speech was far-reaching. In expressing his highest hope that the nation would have that "new birth of freedom," Lincoln remarked that "the world will little note, nor long remember, what we say here."

How very wrong he was.

The Gettysburg Address is now considered, as one speechwriter said, "the crown jewel of American rhetoric," for its brevity, its poetry, its potent push for liberty.

There are five known copies of the Gettysburg

Address written in Lincoln's hand (and with slight differences). Each is named after its recipient. Lincoln gave a copy to Edward Everett; to each of his private secretaries, John Nicolay and John Hay; to historian George Bancroft, who planned to use it in *Autograph Leaves*, a book to serve as a fund-raiser for veterans. The fifth copy went to Colonel Alexander Bliss, publisher of *Autograph Leaves*. Presented here is the Bliss copy. It is the only one that Lincoln signed and is considered to be the standard. And it is the Bliss version that is inscribed in the south chamber of the Lincoln Memorial in Washington, DC.

The world will little note, nor long remember, what we say here, but it can never forget what they did here.

FOUR SCORE AND SEVEN YEARS AGO, OUR FATHERS BROUGHT FORTH UPON THIS CONTINENT A NEW NATION: CONCEIVED IN LIBERTY, AND DEDICATED TO THE PROPOSITION THAT ALL MEN ARE CREATED EQUAL.

Now we are engaged in a great civil war . . . testing whether that nation, or any nation so conceived and so dedicated . . . can long endure. We are met on a great battlefield of that war.

We have come to dedicate a portion of that field as a final resting place for those who here gave their lives that this nation might live. It is altogether fitting and proper that we should do this.

But, in a larger sense, we cannot dedicate . . . we cannot consecrate . . . we cannot hallow this ground. The brave men, living and dead, who struggled here have consecrated it, far above our poor power to add or detract. The world will little note, nor long remember, what we say here, but it can never forget what they did here.

It is for us the living, rather, to be dedicated here to the unfinished work which they who fought here have thus far so nobly advanced. It is rather for us to be here dedicated to the great task remaining before us . . . that from these honored dead we take increased devotion to that cause for which they gave the last full measure of devotion . . . that we here highly resolve that these dead shall not have died in vain . . . that this nation, under God, shall have a new birth of freedom . . . and that government of the people . . . by the people . . . for the people . . . shall not perish from this earth.

THEODORE ROOSEVELT

October 27, 1858–January 6, 1919

SPEECH GIVEN AT THE SORBONNE IN PARIS, FRANCE, 1910

CITIZENSHIP IN A REPUBLIC

THEODORE ROOSEVELT

The credit belongs to the man who is actually in the arena, whose face is marred by dust and sweat and blood. . .

The baker who rises before dawn to prepare quality bread for those who patronize her shop.

The honest butcher who does not put his thumb on the scale in order to cheat a customer out of a few cents.

Stalwart teachers, firefighters, medics, brick-layers, social workers—these are the types of people Theodore Roosevelt commended when he addressed a crowd of more than two thou-sand on April 23, 1910. TR, as he was known, delivered this address at the Sorbonne Univer-sity in Paris, France. The audience included students, military men, and members of the French cabinet.

TR, a powerful orator, was an athlete, sports-man, and naturalist. A hero of the Spanish-American War (1898), he became governor of New York, then vice president of the United States. In 1901, after William McKinley was assassinated, Roosevelt became president. Roosevelt went on to win a second term in 1904. His presidential legacy includes the cre-ation of four national game preserves, fifty-one federal bird reserves, and one hundred fifty national forests. (Theodore "Teddy" Roo-sevelt was once depicted in a cartoon sparing the life of a bear cub, and so teddy bears were named after him.)

After Roosevelt left office in 1908, he went traveling. First he went on a yearlong hunting safari in central Africa with his son Kermit. When he deliv-ered that speech at Paris's Sorbonne, he and his wife, Edith, were touring Europe.

There was much fanfare when the Roo-sevelts arrived at the Sorbonne, which was decked out with a host of American and French flags. An estimated twenty-five thousand peo-ple jammed the streets.

TR wowed the crowd inside the Sorbonne's packed grand amphitheater with a speech that was a bold rebuke of people who complain about things without trying fix problems or help find solutions. He took to task, too, the idle rich in his praise for people who roll up their sleeves and try to make their neighborhood, their city, their state, their nation, their world a healthier, safer, more beautiful place.

Again and again the crowd erupted with mad clapping as Roosevelt delivered this speech, which is sometimes called "The Man in the Arena."

TR was overwhelmed by the reaction to his words. The speech was picked up by newspapers and became an international sensation. Five thousand copies in book form sold within a week.

People from all walks of life and around the globe have quoted from "The Man in the Arena" speech when calling on others to be true citizens of their nations, ready citizens of the world.

TODAY I SHALL SPEAK TO YOU ON THE SUBJECT OF INDIVIDUAL CITIZENSHIP, THE ONE SUBJECT OF VITAL IMPORTANCE TO YOU, MY HEARERS, AND TO ME AND MY COUNTRYMEN, BECAUSE YOU AND WE ARE GREAT CITIZENS OF GREAT DEMOCRATIC REPUBLICS....

With you here, and with us in my own home, in the long run, success or failure will be conditioned upon the way in which the average man, the average woman, does his or her duty, first in the ordinary, every-day affairs of life, and next in those great occasional cries which call for heroic virtues.... Therefore it behooves us to do our best to see that the standard of the average citizen is kept high; and the average cannot be kept high unless the standard of the leaders is very much higher.

It is well if a large proportion of the leaders in any republic, in any democracy, are, as a matter of course, drawn from the classes represented in this audience to-day; but only provided that those classes possess the gifts of sympathy with plain people and of devotion to great ideals....

Let the man of learning, the man of lettered leisure, beware of that queer and cheap temptation to pose to himself and to others as a cynic, as the man who has outgrown emotions and beliefs, the man to whom good and evil are as one. The poorest way to face life is to face it with a sneer. There are many men who feel a kind of twisted pride in cynicism; there are many who confine themselves to criticism of the way others do what they themselves dare not even attempt. There is no more unhealthy being, no man less worthy of respect, than he who either really holds, or feigns to hold, an attitude of sneering disbelief toward all that is great and lofty, whether in achievement or in that noble effort which, even if it fails, comes to second achievement....

It is not the critic who counts; not the man who points out how the strong man stumbles, or where the doer of deeds could have done them better. The credit belongs to the man who is actually in the arena, whose face is marred by dust and sweat and blood; who strives valiantly; who errs, who comes short again and again, because there is no effort without error and shortcoming; but who does actually strive to do the deeds; who knows great enthusiasms, the great devotions; who spends himself in a worthy cause; who at the best knows in the end the triumph of high achievement, and who at the worst, if he fails, at least fails while daring greatly, so that his place shall never be with those cold and timid souls who neither know victory nor defeat.

FRANKLIN DELANO ROOSEVELT

JANUARY 30, 1882–APRIL 12, 1945

FIRST INAUGURAL ADDRESS, 1933

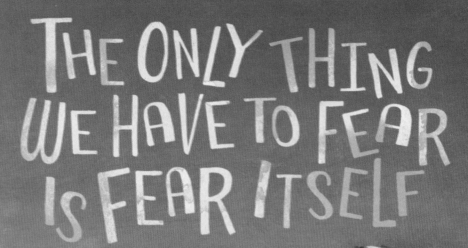

THE ONLY THING WE HAVE TO FEAR IS FEAR ITSELF

FRANKLIN DELANO ROOSEVELT

The October 1929 stock market crash plunged the world into the Great Depression. In weeks and months to come, thousands of American banks failed and millions of people lost all their savings. From hardware stores to mills, hundreds of thousands of businesses went bust. Unemployment skyrocketed. Many people ended up homeless.

In the summer of 1932, some twenty thousand World War I veterans descended upon Washington, DC. These "Bonus Marchers" demanded an early release of the bonuses due them. Other disgruntled, suffering Americans staged hunger marches on state capitals. Still others looted grocery stores.

When Franklin Delano Roosevelt, a distant cousin of Teddy Roosevelt, won the presidency in November 1932, he knew that a great fear gripped the land. Four months later, on Inauguration Day, March 4, 1933, what would he say to a scared, anxious nation? (Inauguration Day was changed to January 20th in 1937.)

DC skies were overcast when FDR, as he was called, took the oath of office on the Capitol's East Portico, then addressed the nation.

Fear not! That was the long and short of FDR's message.

> The only thing we have to fear is fear itself—nameless, unreasoning, unjustified terror which paralyzes needed efforts to convert retreat into advance.

He did not mince words, did not sugarcoat things. He spoke the flat-footed truth. Yes, the nation had hit truly hard times. Yes, America was down.

But not down for the count.

The Great Depression was not the end of the world. The president assured his fellow Americans that the nation would endure, would once again thrive.

Fear not!

FDR knew a thing or two about fear. Born into wealth in Hyde Park, New York, he had lived a very charmed, very active, very easy life until that day in 1921 when he, age thirty-nine, found himself paralyzed from the waist down. (Diagnosis: polio.)

Those were painful, deeply sorrowful days for FDR, but when his spirits lifted, he was a changed man. More compassionate. More serious, too. And this man, who moved mostly in a wheelchair but who trained himself to walk for brief periods with the aid of a cane or crutches after steel braces were strapped onto his legs, became the governor of New York State, a post he held until he won the presidency.

With the help his chief speechwriter, Raymond Moley, FDR had his inaugural address pretty much hammered out a few days before the big day, a day on which he inspired confidence, promising the nation swift and major action to combat what ailed it. FDR more than made good on this promise during this first hundred days in office and beyond, making history as the first US president to win four terms.

During his time in the White House, FDR constantly urged Americans to buck up and to have no fear just as he did on Inauguration Day 1933. FDR's admonition against succumbing to fear has resonated with people facing all kinds of challenges, financial to physical.

THIS IS A DAY OF NATIONAL CONSECRATION, AND I AM CERTAIN THAT MY FELLOW AMERICANS EXPECT THAT ON MY INDUCTION INTO THE PRESIDENCY I WILL ADDRESS THEM WITH A CANDOR AND A DECISION WHICH THE PRESENT SITUATION OF OUR PEOPLE IMPEL.

This is preeminently the time to speak the truth, the whole truth, frankly and boldly. Nor need we shrink from honestly facing conditions in our country today. This great Nation will endure as it has endured, will revive and will prosper.

So, first of all, let me assert my firm belief that the only thing we have to fear is fear itself—nameless, unreasoning, unjustified terror which paralyzes needed efforts to convert retreat into advance.

In every dark hour of our national life a leadership of frankness and vigor has met with that understanding and support of the people themselves which is essential to victory. I am convinced that you will again give that support to leadership in these critical days.

In such a spirit on my part and on yours we face our common difficulties. They concern, thank God, only material things. Values have shrunken to fantastic levels; taxes have risen; our ability to pay has fallen; government of all kinds is faced by serious curtailment of income; the means of exchange are frozen in the currents of trade; the withered leaves of industrial enterprise lie on every side;

FREE SOUP

farmers find no markets for their produce; the savings of many years in thousands of families are gone.

More important, a host of unemployed citizens face the grim problem of existence, and an equally great number toil with little return. Only a foolish optimist can deny the dark realities of the moment.

And yet our distress comes from no failure of substance. We are stricken by no plague of locusts. Compared with the perils which our forefathers conquered because they believed and were not afraid, we have still much to be thankful for. Nature still offers her bounty and human efforts have multiplied it. Plenty is at our doorstep, but a generous use of it languishes in the very sight of the supply. . . .

Our greatest primary task is to put people to work. This is no unsolvable problem if we face it wisely and courageously. It can be accomplished in part by direct recruiting by the Government itself, treating the task as we would treat the emergency of a war, but at the same time, through this employment, accomplishing greatly needed projects to stimulate and reorganize the use of our great natural resources. . . .

And finally, in our progress toward a resumption of work we require two safeguards against a return of the evils of the old order; there must be a strict supervision of all banking and credits and investments; there must be an end to speculation with other people's money, and there must be provision for an adequate but sound currency. . . .

We do not distrust the future of essential democracy. The people of the United States have not failed. In their need they have registered a mandate that they want direct, vigorous action.

They have asked for discipline and direction under leadership. They have made me the present instrument of their wishes. In the spirit of the gift I take it.

In this dedication of a Nation we humbly ask the blessing of God. May He protect each and every one of us. May He guide me in the days to come.

LOU GEHRIG

June 19, 1903–June 2, 1941

SPEECH GIVEN TO THE CROWD
AT YANKEE STADIUM, 1939

FAREWELL TO BASEBALL

LOU GEHRIG

> Today I consider myself the luckiest man on the face of the earth.

*N*ew York Times sportswriter John Drebinger called it "without doubt one of the most touching scenes ever witnessed on a ball field and one that made even case-hardened ball players and chroniclers of the game swallow hard."

The date: Tuesday, July 4, 1939.

The place: The Bronx, New York's Yankee Stadium.

The crowd topped sixty-one thousand on that hot and heavy day of a doubleheader between the New York Yankees and the Washington Senators. More important, it was Lou Gehrig Appreciation Day.

It was after the first game, won by the Senators 3–2, that the Yankees honored their team captain, first baseman Lou Gehrig, nicknamed the "Iron Horse" because he played so hard— even when injured and in great pain.

New York City's feisty mayor, Fiorello La Guardia, and legendary slugger (and former Yankee) George Herman "Babe" Ruth were among the people who sang Lou Gehrig's praises that day. Teammates—sometimes called the Bronx Bombers—and others showered him with gifts. Finally, the plainspoken Iron Horse, with his thick New York accent and trademark humility, took to home plate to say farewell to his beloved sport.

Gehrig had recently been diagnosed with a degenerative disease: amyotrophic lateral sclerosis, ALS for short (now commonly called Lou Gehrig's disease). He had received the diagnosis just weeks earlier, on June 19, his thirty-sixth birthday. "Yet today I consider myself the luckiest man on the face of the earth," he told the crowd at Yankee Stadium.

"The clangy, iron echo of the Yankee stadium, picked up the sentence that poured from the loud speakers and hurled it forth into the world," reported Paul Gallico. "'The luckiest man on the face of the earth . . . luckiest man on the face of the earth . . . luckiest man . . .'"

This luckiest man, this gentle giant, was a native New Yorker, born Heinrich Ludwig Gehrig to German immigrants on the fifty-seventh anniversary of the first known organized baseball game.

When Gehrig delivered his farewell address, he held the record for the most consecutive games ever played: 2,130 (a record not broken until 1995 by Baltimore Orioles shortstop Cal Ripken Jr.). Gehrig's other laurels during his seventeen years as a Yankee include twice being named the American League's Most Valuable Player and being part of a team that won the World Series six times. Gehrig had a batting average of .340 and 493 career home runs, a total that could have been much higher had his life not ended shortly.

In his farewell address, Gehrig was grateful and counting his blessings: both his fans and his fellow Yankees, including the team's recently deceased owner, Jacob Ruppert. Also on the list, his parents, his mother-in-law, and his wife of eight years, Chicago socialite Eleanor Twitchell.

At points the crowd shouted, "We love you, Lou!"

At points he choked up.

Could he make it through?

He did.

And by the way, the Yankees won game two, 11–1.

Months later, in December 1939, the Iron Horse was inducted into the Baseball Hall of Fame. Also, his number—number 4—was retired, a first for a major league baseball player.

Nearly a year and a half later and shortly before his thirty-eighth birthday, Lou Gehrig died in his home at 5204 Delafield Avenue in the Riverdale section of the Bronx.

Down through the years, Lou Gehrig's farewell speech has inspired people from all walks of life to not give in to self-pity when faced with a "bad break," to remember that when the going gets tough, the tough get grateful.

Some have hailed Gehrig's speech the Gettysburg Address of baseball.

I might have been given a bad break, but I've got an awful lot to live for.

FANS, FOR THE PAST TWO WEEKS YOU HAVE BEEN READING ABOUT A BAD BREAK I GOT. YET TODAY I CONSIDER MYSELF THE LUCKIEST MAN ON THE FACE OF THE EARTH.

I have been in ballparks for seventeen years and have never received anything but kindness and encouragement from you fans. Look at these grand men. Which of you wouldn't consider it the highlight of his career just to associate with them for even one day?

Sure I'm lucky.

Who wouldn't consider it an honor to have known Jacob Ruppert? Also, the builder of baseball's greatest empire, Ed Barrow? To have spent six years with that wonderful little fellow, Miller Huggins? Then to have spent the next nine years with that outstanding leader, that smart student of psychology, the best manager in baseball today, Joe McCarthy?

Sure I'm lucky.

When the New York Giants, a team you would give your right arm to beat, and vice versa, sends you a gift—that's something. When everybody down to the groundskeepers and those boys in white coats remember you with trophies— that's something.

When you have a wonderful mother-in-law who takes sides with you in squabbles with her own daughter— that's something.

When you have a father and a mother who work all their lives so you can have an education and build your body—it's a blessing.

When you have a wife who has been a tower of strength and shown more courage than you dreamed existed—that's the finest I know.

So, I close in saying that I might have been given a bad break, but I've got an awful lot to live for.

LANGSTON HUGHES

FEBRUARY 1, 1902–MAY 22, 1967

SPEECH TO THE NATIONAL ASSEMBLY
OF AUTHORS AND DRAMATISTS, 1957

ON THE BLACKLIST ALL OUR LIVES

LANGSTON HUGHES

On May 7, 1957, the fifty-five-year-old poet, playwright, novelist, and social activist Langston Hughes, a native of Joplin, Missouri, appeared on the panel "The Writer's Position in America." This was at New York City's Alvin Theatre, at an event sponsored by the Authors' League of America.

Langston Hughes had graduated from Lincoln University in Pennsylvania, the school once known as "the black Princeton." By the 1950s, Hughes was one of the best-known, most successful American writers. One of the innovators of poetry inspired by and rooted in the blues and jazz music, and also star of an artistic movement often called the Harlem Renaissance, Hughes had catapulted to fame in 1926 with the publication of his collection of poetry *The Weary Blues*. By then, Hughes, who as child and a teen had lived in several American cities (including Lawrence, Kansas; Topeka, Kansas; Cleveland, Ohio; and Washington, DC), had held down all kinds of jobs while waiting for that big break. He had been a truck farmer, a delivery boy, a busboy, a cook, a waiter. He had even had a stint as an assistant to Carter G. Woodson, the "Father of Black History." Hughes had also seen some

of the world as a sailor. That included some of France, Holland, Italy, Mexico, Portugal, and several countries in West Africa. All the while, he wrote! wrote! wrote! In 1924, two years before *Weary Blues* came out, Hughes made Harlem home.

The 1957 New York City panel Hughes took part in came in the aftermath of the second Red Scare (1946–1956). This was a time of great persecution of Americans known to be or thought to be "Reds"; that is, Communists: people who believed in the economic, social, and political ideologies of America's archenemy, the Soviet Union. Many Americans, from federal government employees to Hollywood screenwriters, were investigated and subjected to Congressional hearings. They led to imprisonment for some.

More men and women, Communists and not, wound up on the "blacklist"; that is, they were shunned, ostracized. For example, the

> Negro writers, just by being black, have been on the blacklist all our lives.

only way some blacklisted screenwriters got work was by writing under aliases.

In 1953, Langston Hughes had come before one of those Congressional hearings. Out of fear, he denounced his writings regarded as radical and said that his sympathies for the Soviet ideology had ended a few years earlier.

While the anti-Communist hysteria had waned when Langston Hughes spoke at the Alvin Theatre in 1957, there was still a chill in the air and concern about the writers being censored; that is, forced to delete things from their work in order to get published or produced.

Censorship was nothing new for the black writer, Hughes pointed out. He stressed how difficult it was for most black writers to get their manuscripts published or their plays staged by white-owned outlets. Black writers simply did not have the same access as white ones.

With references to Autherine Lucy's battle to be the first black person to attend the University of Alabama (1956), the bombing of Martin Luther King Jr.'s home because of his work on the bus boycott in Montgomery, Alabama (1955–1956), and the lynching of fourteen-year-old Emmett Till in Money, Mississippi (1955), Hughes reminded the audience that for so many blacks in America, liberty was still a dream deferred. Cut off from so many opportunities, they were on a blacklist, so to speak.

Hughes ended his address with a poem about a black child's anxiety because of Jim Crow, as segregation is commonly called. The US Supreme Court ruled that segregation was constitutional back in 1896, in the case *Plessy v. Ferguson*. The *Plessy* decision was essentially overturned years later by a different group of US Supreme Court justices in the case *Brown v. Board of Education*. The *Brown* decision was handed down on May 17 1954. Though no longer government-sanctioned, Jim Crow remained very much alive for years to come. And Americans of African descent remained on the blacklist, in many realms of life, some until the day they died.

BRUCE CATTON SPOKE TODAY OF THE WRITER'S CHANCE TO BE HEARD. MY CHANCE TO BE HEARD, AS A NEGRO WRITER, IS NOT SO GREAT AS YOUR CHANCE, IF YOU ARE WHITE. I ONCE APPROACHED THE PLAY SERVICE OF THE DRAMATISTS GUILD AS TO THE HANDLING OF SOME OF MY PLAYS. *NO, WAS THE ANSWER,* THEY WOULD NOT KNOW WHERE TO PLACE PLAYS ABOUT NEGRO LIFE.

I once sent one of my best known short stories, before it came out in book form, to one of our oldest and foremost American magazines. The story was about racial violence in the South. It came back to me with a very brief little note saying the editor did not believe his readers wished to read about such things.

Another story of mine which did not concern race problems at all came back to me from one of our best known editors of anthologies of fiction with a letter praising the story but saying that he, the editor, could not tell if the characters were white or colored. Would I make them definitely Negro? Just a plain story about human beings from me was not up his alley, it seems. So before the word *man* I simply inserted *black,* and before the girl's name, the words *brownskin*—and the story was accepted. Only a mild form of racial bias. But now let us come to something more serious.

Censorship, the Black List: Negro writers, just by being black, have been on the blacklist all our lives. Do you know that there are libraries in our country that will not stock a book by a Negro writer, not even as a gift? There are towns where Negro newspapers and magazines cannot be sold except surreptitiously. There are American magazines that have never published anything by Negroes. There are film studios that have never hired a Negro writer. Censorship for us begins at the color line.

We have in America today about a dozen top flight, frequently published, and really good Negro writers. Do you not think it strange that of that dozen, at least half of them live abroad, far away from their people, their problems, and the sources of their material: . . . in Paris . . . in Rome . . . in Southern France and . . . in Mexico.

Why? Because the stones thrown at Autherine Lucy at the University of Alabama are thrown at them, too. Because the shadow of Montgomery and the bombs under Rev. King's house, shadow them and shatter them, too. Because the body of little Emmett Till drowned in a Mississippi River and no one brought to justice, haunts them, too. One of the writers I've mentioned, when last I saw him before he went abroad, said to me, "I don't want my children to grow up in the shadow of Jim Crow."

And so let us end with children. And let us end with . . . a poem. It's about a child—a little colored child. I imagine her as being maybe six or seven years old. She grew up in the Deep South where our color lines are still legal. Then her family moved to a Northern or Western industrial city—one of those continual migrations of Negroes looking for a better town. There in this Northern city—maybe a place like Newark, New Jersey, or Omaha, Nebraska, or Oakland, California, the little girl goes one day to a carnival, and she sees the merry-go-round going around, and she wants to ride. But being a little colored child, and remembering the South, she doesn't know if she can ride or not. And if she can ride, where? So this is what she says:

Where is the Jim Crow section
On this merry-go-round,
Mister, cause I want to ride?
Down South where I come from
White and colored
Can't sit side by side.
Down South on the train
There's a Jim Crow car.
On the bus we're put in the back—
But there ain't no back
To a merry-go-round!
Where's the horse
For a kid that's black?

JOHN FITZGERALD KENNEDY

MAY 29, 1917–NOVEMBER 22, 1963

ADDRESS AT RICE UNIVERSITY,
HOUSTON, TEXAS, 1962

WE CHOOSE TO GO TO THE MOON

JOHN FITZGERALD KENNEDY

On October 4, 1957, the Soviet Union successfully launched the first artificial satellite, *Sputnik 1*, ushering in the Space Age.

The Space Race, too.

The United States bristled over the idea of the Soviet Union, its enemy at the time, having a monopoly on space exploration. In the summer of 1958, President Dwight D. Eisenhower signed into law an act that created the National Aeronautics and Space Administration (NASA). Its mission: to get American astronauts into space.

A few years later, on April 12, 1961, the Soviet Union's Yuri Gagarin, aboard *Vostok 1*, became the first human being to orbit the Earth. Gagarin's historic flight occurred twenty-three days before NASA's Alan Shepard achieved suborbital flight aboard *Freedom 7*. Not until February 20, 1962, did an American take off for outer space. That was John Glenn. His spacecraft was *Friendship 7*.

Later that year, America's thirty-fifth president, John F. Kennedy, embarked on a four-city tour to promote his great ambition to land an American on the moon by the end of the 1960s, a goal he had announced back in May

> We set sail on this new sea because there is new knowledge to be gained, and new rights to be won, and they must be won and used for the progress of all people.

1961. The moon mission, Apollo, was named after the Greek god Apollo by a NASA founder, Dr. Abe Silverstein. The image of "Apollo riding his chariot across the sun was appropriate to the grand scale of the proposed program," he later said.

President Kennedy's best-known address during that four-city tour occurred on September 12, 1962, in Houston, Texas, in the Rice University stadium. Some fifty thousand people filled the stands.

There had been great grumbling in the nation about the cost of the space program. But Kennedy, a gifted speaker, was determined.

In his speech at Rice, he defended the space program and did his utmost to rally the crowd in the stadium and millions of other Americans to get behind his dream of landing an American on the moon.

After his roughly thirty-minute speech at Rice, the president toured NASA's new Manned Spacecraft Center in Houston (now the Johnson Space Center). There he was shown a mock-up of "the Bug," as the lunar lander was called. He also received a miniature model of the command module, Apollo.

JFK, as the president was known, got his wish.

Support for the moon mission soared. The government ended up pumping more than $25 billion into the endeavor. And NASA made history: the United States became the first nation to get astronauts to the moon. It happened with the voyage of *Apollo 11*.

The first person to set foot on the moon was *Apollo 11*'s mission commander, Neil Armstrong. On July 20, 1969, Armstrong made his famous "one small step," which signaled "one giant leap" for human beings.

Sadly, JFK never lived to see this milestone moment. He had been assassinated in November 1963, a little over a year after his speech at Rice Stadium.

And it is a speech that still heartens people today because it is essentially a tribute to the American can-do spirit.

But why, some say, the moon? Why choose this as our goal? And they may well ask why climb the highest mountain? . . .

...DESPITE THE STRIKING FACT THAT MOST OF THE SCIENTISTS THAT THE WORLD HAS EVER KNOWN ARE ALIVE AND WORKING TODAY, DESPITE THE FACT THAT THIS NATION'S OWN SCIENTIFIC MANPOWER IS DOUBLING EVERY 12 YEARS IN A RATE OF GROWTH MORE THAN THREE TIMES THAT OF OUR POPULATION AS A WHOLE, DESPITE THAT, THE VAST STRETCHES OF THE UNKNOWN AND THE UNANSWERED AND THE UNFINISHED STILL FAR OUTSTRIP OUR COLLECTIVE COMPREHENSION.

No man can fully grasp how far and how fast we have come, but condense, if you will, the 50,000 years of man's recorded history in a time span of but a half-century. Stated in these terms, we know very little about the first 40 years, except at the end of them advanced man had learned to use the skins of animals to cover them. Then about 10 years ago, under this standard, man emerged from his caves to construct other kinds of shelter. Only five years ago man learned to write and use a cart with wheels. Christianity began less than two years ago. The printing press came this year, and then less than two months ago, during this whole 50-year span of human history, the steam engine provided a new source of power.

Newton explored the meaning of gravity. Last month electric lights and telephones and automobiles and airplanes became available. Only last week did we develop penicillin and television and nuclear power, and now if America's new spacecraft succeeds in reaching Venus, we will have literally reached the stars before midnight tonight.

This is a breathtaking pace, and such a pace cannot help but create new ills as it dispels old, new ignorance, new problems, new dangers. Surely the opening vistas of space promise high costs and hardships, as well as high reward. . . .

If this capsule history of our progress teaches us anything, it is that man, in his quest for knowledge and progress, is determined and cannot be deterred. The exploration of space will go ahead, whether we join in it or not, and it is one of the great adventures of all time, and no nation which expects to be the leader of other nations can expect to stay behind in the race for space.

Those who came before us made certain that this country rode the first waves of the industrial revolutions, the first waves of modern invention, and the first wave of nuclear power, and this generation does not intend to founder in the backwash of the coming age of space. We mean to be a part of it—we mean to lead it. For the eyes of the world now look into space, to the moon and to the planets beyond, and we have vowed that we shall not see it governed by a hostile flag of conquest, but by a banner of freedom and peace. We have vowed that we shall not see space filled with weapons of mass destruction, but with instruments of knowledge and understanding.

Yet the vows of this Nation can only be fulfilled if we in this Nation are first, and, therefore, we intend to be first.

We set sail on this new sea because there is new knowledge to be gained, and new rights to be won, and they must be won and used for the progress of all people. For space science, like nuclear science and all technology, has no conscience of its own. Whether it will become a force for good or ill depends on man, and only if the United States occupies a position of pre-eminence can we help decide whether this new ocean will be a sea of peace or a new terrifying theater of war. I do not say that we should or will go unprotected against the hostile misuse of space any more than we go unprotected against the hostile use of land or sea, but I do say that space can be explored and mastered without feeding the fires of war, without repeating the mistakes that man has made in extending his writ around this globe of ours.

There is no strife, no prejudice, no national conflict in outer space as yet. Its hazards are hostile to us all. Its conquest deserves the best of all mankind, and its opportunity for peaceful cooperation may never come again. But why, some say, the moon? Why choose this as our goal? And they may well ask why climb the highest mountain? . . .

We choose to go to the moon. We choose to go to the moon in this decade and do the other things, not because they are easy, but because they are hard,

because that goal will serve to organize and measure the best of our energies and skills, because that challenge is one that we are willing to accept, one we are unwilling to postpone, and one which we intend to win, and the others, too. . . .

In the last 24 hours we have seen facilities now being created for the greatest and most complex exploration in man's history. We have felt the ground shake and the air shattered by the testing of a Saturn C-1 booster rocket, many times as powerful as the Atlas which launched John Glenn, generating power equivalent to 10,000 automobiles with their accelerators on the floor. We have seen the site where the F-1 rocket engines, each one as powerful as all eight engines of the Saturn combined, will be clustered together to make the advanced Saturn missile, assembled in a new building to be built at Cape Canaveral as tall as a 48 story structure, as wide as a city block, and as long as two lengths of this field.

Within these last 19 months at least 45 satellites have circled the earth. Some 40 of them were "made in the United States of America" and they were far more sophisticated and supplied far more knowledge to the people of the world than those of the Soviet Union.

The *Mariner* spacecraft now on its way to Venus is the most intricate instrument in the history of space science. The accuracy of that shot is comparable to firing a missile from Cape Canaveral and dropping it in this stadium between the 40-yard lines.

Transit satellites are helping our ships at sea to steer a safer course. Tiros satellites have given us unprecedented warnings of hurricanes and storms, and will do the same for forest fires and icebergs.

We have had our failures, but so have others, even if they do not admit them. And they may be less public.

To be sure, we are behind, and will be behind for some time in manned flight. But we do not intend to stay behind, and in this decade, we shall make up and move ahead. . . .

Many years ago the great British explorer George Mallory, who was to die on Mount Everest, was asked why did he want to climb it. He said, "Because it is there."

Well, space is there, and we're going to climb it, and the moon and the planets are there, and new hopes for knowledge and peace are there. And, therefore, as we set sail we ask God's blessing on the most hazardous and dangerous and greatest adventure on which man has ever embarked.

MARTIN LUTHER KING JR.

January 15, 1929–April 4, 1968

SPEECH AT THE MARCH ON WASHINGTON FOR JOBS AND FREEDOM, 1963

I HAVE A DREAM

MARTIN LUTHER KING JR.

> Let freedom ring from every hill. . . . Let freedom ring.

"Tell them about your dream, Martin! Tell them about the dream!"

On Wednesday, August 28, 1963, in a sweltering Washington, DC, some two hundred and fifty thousand people, most of them black, gathered at the National Mall in a peaceful protest called the March on Washington for Jobs and Freedom.

At the march, the focal point was the memorial to Abraham Lincoln, who had issued the Emancipation Proclamation a hundred years earlier.

Speakers included black labor leader A. Philip Randolph, one of the march's organizers, and white labor leader Walter Reuther. The final speaker was thirty-four-year-old Martin Luther King Jr., son, grandson, and great-grandson of Baptist preachers—a master of stirring, soaring Baptist-style preaching.

The native of Atlanta, Georgia, was the most high-profile of the civil rights leaders. And so much more than that. King's ultimate dream was the Beloved Community—justice for all and harmony among all. "The end is reconciliation; the end is redemption; the end is the creation of the beloved community," said King at the end of the successful 1955–

1956 Montgomery Bus Boycott, which Rosa Parks had inspired and he had led.

Seven years later, at the March on Washington, standing on the steps of the Lincoln Memorial, King was midway through his address when the mighty gospel singer Mahalia Jackson, seated on the dais, called out, "Tell them about your dream, Martin! Tell them about the dream!"

King abandoned his prepared remarks. Instead he spontaneously delivered a speech that he had delivered before—one with the refrain "I have a dream." King had been inspired to write this speech after hearing a sermon by Prathia Hall in September 1962. Hall was preaching at a church in Georgia that had been rebuilt after the Ku Klux Klan burned it down. In her sermon, Prathia Hall repeated the words

"I have a dream." These words got wings at the March on Washington.

King's poignant speech, along with the others—indeed, the whole March on Washington—led to the Civil Rights Act passed by Congress and signed into law by President Lyndon Johnson in 1964.

"I Have a Dream" is without a doubt Martin Luther King Jr.'s best-known, most popular speech, but it would be a grave mistake to think that you can understand his "dream" from just this speech. After you have read "I Have a Dream," a fine introduction to his oratory, consider reading more of him.

AM HAPPY TO JOIN WITH YOU TODAY IN WHAT WILL GO DOWN IN HISTORY AS THE GREATEST DEMONSTRATION FOR FREEDOM IN THE HISTORY OF OUR NATION.

Five score years ago a great American in whose symbolic shadow we stand today signed the Emancipation Proclamation. This momentous decree came as a great beacon light of hope to millions of Negro slaves who had been seared in the flames of withering injustice. It came as a joyous daybreak to end the long night of their captivity. But one hundred years later, the Negro still is not free. One hundred years later, the life of the Negro is still sadly crippled by the manacles of segregation and the chains of discrimination. One hundred years later, the Negro lives on a lonely island of poverty in the midst of a vast ocean of material prosperity. One hundred years later, the Negro is still languished in the corners of American society and finds himself an exile in his own land. So we've come here today to dramatize a shameful condition.

In a sense we have come to our nation's capital to cash a check. When the architects of our Republic wrote the magnificent words of the Constitution and the Declaration of Independence, they were signing a promissory note to which every American was to fall heir. This note was a promise that all men—yes, black men as well as white men—would be guaranteed the unalienable rights of life,

liberty and the pursuit of happiness. It is obvious today that America has defaulted on this promissory note insofar as her citizens of color are concerned. Instead of honoring this sacred obligation, America has given the Negro people a bad check, a check which has come back marked "insufficient funds."

But we refuse to believe that the bank of justice is bankrupt. We refuse to believe that there are insufficient funds in the great vaults of opportunity of this nation. So we've come to cash this check, a check that will give us upon demand the riches of freedom and the security of justice.

We have also come to this hallowed spot to remind America of the fierce urgency of now. This is no time to engage in the luxury of cooling off or to take the tranquilizing drug of gradualism. Now is the time to make real the promises of democracy. Now is the time to rise from the dark and desolate valley of segregation to the sunlit path of racial justice. Now is the time to lift our nation from the quicksands of racial injustice to the solid rock of brotherhood.

Now is the time to make justice a reality for all of God's children. It would be fatal for the nation to overlook the urgency of the moment. This sweltering summer of the Negro's legitimate discontent will not pass until there is an invigorating autumn of freedom and equality—1963 is not an end, but a beginning. Those who hope that the Negro needed to blow off steam and will now be content will have a rude awakening if the nation returns to business as usual.

There will be neither rest nor tranquility in America until the Negro is granted his citizenship rights. The whirlwinds of revolt will continue to shake the foundations of our nation until the bright day of justice emerges. But there is something that I must say to my people who stand on the warm threshold which leads into the palace of justice. In the process of gaining our rightful place we must not be guilty of wrongful deeds. Let us not seek to satisfy our thirst for freedom by drinking from the cup of bitterness and hatred.

We must forever conduct our struggle on the high plane of dignity and discipline. We must not allow our creative protest to degenerate into physical violence. Again and again we must rise to the majestic heights of meeting physical force with soul force. The marvelous new militancy which has engulfed the Negro community must not lead us to distrust all white people, for many of our white brothers, as evidenced by their presence here today, have come to realize that their destiny is tied up with our destiny.

They have come to realize that their freedom is inextricably bound to our freedom. We cannot walk alone. And as we walk, we must make the pledge that we shall always march ahead. We cannot turn back. There are those who are asking the devotees of civil rights, "When will you be satisfied?" We can never be satisfied as long as the Negro is the victim of all the unspeakable horrors of police brutality.

We can never be satisfied, as long as our bodies, heavy with the fatigue of travel, cannot gain lodging in the motels of the highways and the hotels of the cities.

We cannot be satisfied as long as the Negro's basic mobility is from a smaller ghetto to a larger one. We can never be satisfied as long as our children are stripped of their selfhood and robbed of their dignity by signs stating "For Whites Only."

We cannot be satisfied as long as a Negro in Mississippi cannot vote and a Negro in New York believes he has nothing for which to vote.

No, no, we are not satisfied, and we will not be satisfied until justice rolls down like waters and righteousness like a mighty stream.

I am not unmindful that some of you have come here out of great trials and tribulations. Some of you have come fresh from narrow jail cells. Some of you have come from areas where your quest for freedom left you battered by the storms of persecution and staggered by the winds of police brutality. You have been the veterans of creative suffering.

Continue to work with the faith that unearned suffering is redemptive. Go back to Mississippi, go back to Alabama, go back to South Carolina, go back to Georgia, go back to Louisiana, go back to the slums and ghettos of our northern cities, knowing that somehow this situation can and will be changed. Let us not wallow in the valley of despair.

I say to you today, my friends, so even though we face the difficulties of today and tomorrow, I still have a dream. It is a dream deeply rooted in the American dream. I have a dream that one day this nation will rise up and live out the true meaning of its creed: "We hold these truths to be self-evident, that all men are created equal."

I have a dream that one day on the red hills of Georgia the sons of former slaves and the sons of former slave owners will be able to sit down together at the table of brotherhood. I have a dream that one day even the state of Mississippi, a state sweltering with the heat of injustice, sweltering with the heat of oppression, will be transformed into an oasis of freedom and justice.

I have a dream that my four little chil-dren will one day live in a nation where they will not be judged by the color of their skin but by the content of their character. I have a dream today. I have a dream that one day down in Alabama, with its vicious racists, with its governor having his lips dripping with the words of interposition and nullification; one day right there in Alabama, little black boys and black girls will be able to join hands with little white boys and white girls as sisters and brothers.

I have a dream today. I have a dream that one day every valley shall be exalted, every hill and mountain shall be made low, the rough places will be made plain, and the crooked places will be made straight. And the glory of the Lord shall be revealed, and all flesh shall see it together. This is our hope. This is the faith that I go back to the South with. With this faith we will be able to hew out of the mountain of despair a stone of hope. With this faith we will be able to transform the jangling discords of our nation into a beautiful symphony of brotherhood. With this faith we will be able to work together, to pray together, to struggle together, to go to jail together, to stand up for freedom together, knowing that we will be free one day.

This will be the day when all of God's children will be able to sing with new meaning, "My country, 'tis of thee, sweet land of liberty, of thee I sing. Land where my fathers died, land of the pilgrim's pride, from every mountainside, let freedom ring." And if America is to be a great nation, this must become true. So let freedom ring from the prodigious hilltops of New Hampshire. Let freedom ring from the mighty mountains of New York. Let freedom ring from the heightening Alleghenies of Pennsylvania. Let freedom ring from the snowcapped Rockies of Colorado. Let freedom ring from the curvaceous slopes of California.

But not only that. Let freedom ring from Stone Mountain of Georgia. Let freedom ring from Lookout Mountain of Tennessee. Let freedom ring from every hill and molehill of Mississippi, from every mountain side. Let freedom ring. . . .

And when this happens, when we allow freedom ring—when we let it ring from every village and every hamlet, from every state and every city, we will be able to speed up that day when all of God's children, black men and white men, Jews and Gentiles, Protestants and Catholics, will be able to join hands and sing in the words of the old Negro spiritual, "Free at last, Free at last, Thank God Almighty, We are free at last."

FANNIE LOU HAMER

October 6, 1917–March 14, 1977

**TESTIMONY BEFORE THE CREDENTIALS COMMITTEE,
DEMOCRATIC NATIONAL CONVENTION, 1964**

I QUESTION AMERICA

FANNIE LOU HAMER

It was the 31st of August of 1962 that eighteen of us traveled twenty-six miles to the county courthouse in Indianola to try to register to become first-class citizens.

Childhood polio left her, the youngest of her parents' twenty children, with a limp. Poverty, rooted in racism, meant that at a young age she had to leave school to work the land her family sharecropped. She later married a man who was a sharecropper, too.

No one would have predicted that Fannie Lou Hamer would ever make a name for herself, ever appear on the national stage, or emerge as one of the greatest, strongest voices for freedom during the modern civil rights movement.

Freedom from ramshackle schools.

Freedom from low-paying jobs.

Freedom from white terrorist organizations such as the Ku Klux Klan.

Freedom to vote.

In August 1962, with a band of brave black women and men, forty-four-year-old Fannie Lou Hamer of Ruleville, Mississippi, boarded a bus to nearby Indianola. Their aim: to register to vote.

Black men had received the national vote back in 1870. Women in 1920. But over the years black voter suppression was a constant, especially in the South. Millions of black Americans were denied their right to vote through trickery, intimidation, and raw violence. On that August 1962 day when Fannie Lou Hamer and her colleagues attempted to register, they were thwarted by a literacy test to which whites were not subjected.

Freedom to have a child. That was also a concern of Fannie Lou Hamer. Back in 1961, when she went to the county hospital for a minor procedure, she was given another one that she had not signed up for. She was sterilized. She later reckoned that six out of every ten black women who went to that hospital were given an operation—without their consent—that would prevent them from ever having a baby.

It was partly her stolen freedom to have

a child that radicalized Hamer, led to her boarding that bus to Indianola, led her to not giving up on her right to vote.

Though her family was evicted from the plantation on which they worked, though her life was threatened numerous times, Fannie Lou Hamer persevered. Eventually she passed that darned literacy test.

Hamer went on to help others ready themselves for the test. She also joined the Student Nonviolent Coordinating Committee (SNCC), an organization formed by young people in the forefront of the sit-in movement. Hamer was a founder of SNCC's Mississippi Freedom Democratic Party (MFDP), an interracial political party created as an alternative to the Magnolia State's Democratic Party, which was composed of mostly white segregationists.

It was for the cause of MFDP that in August 1964, Fannie Lou Hamer traveled to Atlantic City, New Jersey, host of that year's Democratic National Convention. Her aim was to convince the party's credentials committee to recognize the MFDP.

Hamer's testimony included some of the trials and tribulations she had suffered during her freedom quest. For one thing, there was a jailhouse beating that left her with a blood clot in her left eye and a damaged kidney. And her testimony was televised.

President Lyndon Johnson was furious over Hamer's speech, furious over the MFDP's existence. He feared that if the party was recognized (which didn't happen), legions of white Southerners would throw their support behind his Republican opponent in the upcoming election, Barry Goldwater. Johnson had worked hard to get President Kennedy's civil rights bill enacted into law—a law that outlawed discrimination in public places, which Johnson had signed in July 1964. And the president had more civil rights legislation he wanted Congress to pass.

To knock Hamer off the airways, Johnson held an impromptu press conference.

His ploy backfired. Networks found Hamer's testimony so compelling that they aired it that evening, giving that light of hers, that courage of hers, an even larger audience.

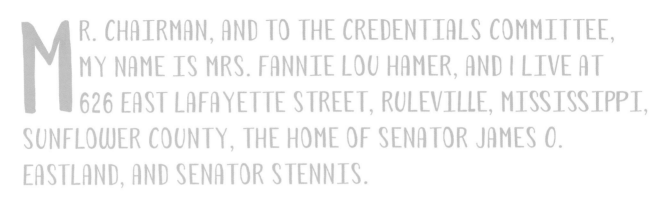

MR. CHAIRMAN, AND TO THE CREDENTIALS COMMITTEE, MY NAME IS MRS. FANNIE LOU HAMER, AND I LIVE AT 626 EAST LAFAYETTE STREET, RULEVILLE, MISSISSIPPI, SUNFLOWER COUNTY, THE HOME OF SENATOR JAMES O. EASTLAND, AND SENATOR STENNIS.

It was the 31st of August of 1962 that eighteen of us traveled twenty-six miles to the county courthouse in Indianola to try to register to become first-class citizens.

We was met in Indianola by police-men, highway patrolmen, and they only allowed two of us in to take the literacy test at the time. After we had taken this test and started back to Ruleville, we was held up by the city police and the state highway patrolmen and carried back to Indianola where the

bus driver was charged that day with driving a bus the wrong color.

After we paid the fine among us, we continued on to Ruleville, and Reverend Jeff Sunny carried me four miles in the rural area where I had worked as a time-keeper and sharecropper for eighteen years. I was met there by my children, who told me that the plantation owner was angry because I had gone down to try to register.

After they told me, my husband came, and said the plantation owner was raising Cain because I had tried to register. Before he quit talking the plantation owner came and said, "Fannie Lou, do you know—did Pap tell you what I said?"

And I said, "Yes, sir."

He said, "Well I mean that." He said, "If you don't go down and withdraw your registration, you will have to leave." Said, "Then if you go down and withdraw," said, "you still might have to go because we are not ready for that in Mississippi."

And I addressed him and told him and said, "I didn't try to register for you. I tried to register for myself."

I had to leave that same night.

On the 10th of September 1962, sixteen bullets was fired into the home of Mr. and Mrs. Robert Tucker for me. That same night two girls were shot in Ruleville, Mississippi. Also Mr. Joe McDonald's house was shot in.

And June the 9th, 1963, I had attended a voter registration workshop; was returning back to Mississippi. Ten of us was traveling by the Continental Trailway bus. When we got to Winona, Mississippi, which is Montgomery County, four of the people got off to use the washroom, and two of the people—to use the restaurant—two of the people wanted to use the washroom.

The four people that had gone in to use the restaurant was ordered out.

All of this on account of we want to register, to become first-class citizens.

During this time I was on the bus. But when I looked through the window and saw they had rushed out I got off of the bus to see what had happened. And one of the ladies said, "It was a State Highway Patrolman and a Chief of Police ordered us out."

I got back on the bus and one of the persons had used the washroom got back on the bus, too.

As soon as I was seated on the bus, I saw when they began to get the five people in a highway patrolman's car. I stepped off of the bus to see what was happening and somebody screamed from the car that the five workers was in and said, "Get that one there." When I went to get in the car, when the man told me I was under arrest, he kicked me.

I was carried to the county jail and

> Is this America,
> the land of the free
> and the home of the brave,
> where we have to sleep with
> our telephones off the hooks
> because our lives be threatened
> daily, because we want to live
> as decent human beings,
> in America?

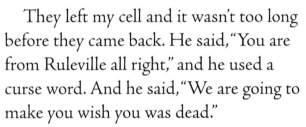

put in the booking room. They left some of the people in the booking room and began to place us in cells. I was placed in a cell with a young woman called Miss Ivesta Simpson. After I was placed in the cell I began to hear sounds of licks and screams, I could hear the sounds of licks and horrible screams. . . .

And they would say other horrible names.

She would say, "Yes, I can say 'yes, sir.'"

"So, well, say it."

She said, "I don't know you well enough."

They beat her, I don't know how long. And after a while she began to pray, and asked God to have mercy on those people.

And it wasn't too long before three white men came to my cell. One of these men was a State Highway Patrolman and he asked me where I was from. I told him Ruleville and he said, "We are going to check this."

They left my cell and it wasn't too long before they came back. He said, "You are from Ruleville all right," and he used a curse word. And he said, "We are going to make you wish you was dead."

I was carried out of that cell into another cell where they had two Negro prisoners. The State Highway Patrolmen ordered the first Negro to take the blackjack.

The first Negro prisoner ordered me, by orders from the State Highway Patrolman, for me to lay down on a bunk bed on my face.

I laid on my face and the first Negro began to beat. I was beat by the first Negro until he was exhausted. I was holding my hands behind me at that time on my left side, because I suffered from polio when I was six years old.

After the first Negro had beat until he was exhausted, the State Highway Patrolman ordered the second Negro to take the blackjack.

The second Negro began to beat and I began to work my feet, and the State Highway Patrolman ordered the first Negro who had beat me to sit on my feet—to keep me from working my feet. I began to scream and one white man got up and began to beat me in my head and tell me to hush.

One white man—my dress had worked up high—he walked over and pulled my dress—I pulled my dress down and he pulled my dress back up.

I was in jail when Medgar Evers was murdered.

All of this is on account of we want to register, to become first-class citizens. And if the Freedom Democratic Party is not seated now, I question America. Is this America, the land of the free and the home of the brave, where we have to sleep with our telephones off the hooks because our lives be threatened daily, because we want to live as decent human beings, in America?

Thank you.

CESAR CHAVEZ

MARCH 31, 1927–APRIL 23, 1993

ADDRESS TO THE COMMONWEALTH CLUB OF CALIFORNIA, 1984

CESAR CHAVEZ

> Once social change begins, it cannot be reversed. You cannot uneducate the person who has learned to read. You cannot humiliate the person who feels pride. You cannot oppress the people who are not afraid anymore.

"The dark brown man's deep sad eyes scanned the roomful of San Francisco's wealthy and worldly. Few assembled in the gilded splendor of the Sheraton-Palace Hotel on the fall day in 1984 had seen a lettuce field, or a farmworker bent over in pain. They had all seen the face of Cesar Chavez."

So begins the prologue to Miriam Pawel's biography of the dark brown Mexican American with deep sad eyes, who, with Dolores Huerta, cofounded the National Farm Workers Association in 1962, a union that eventually became the United Farm Workers.

Their mission: to fight for the rights of California's migrant agricultural workers, with a focus on those who toiled for the growers of lettuce, grapes, and tomatoes. These workers, mostly Mexicans and Filipinos (with children among them), spent long, body-breaking hours planting and reaping for a pittance. They were given horrible housing. They were subjected to violence for the least infraction. All this so that Americans could enjoy cheap fruits and vegetables.

Arizona-born Cesar Chavez truly understood the plight of the migrant agricultural workers. He had been one.

The problem was not confined to California. When Chavez cofounded his union, it had been only two years since CBS broadcast, on Thanksgiving Day, Edward R. Murrow's documentary *Harvest of Shame*, an exposé on the hellish lives of roughly three million migrant farm workers, most of whom earned a mere $900 a year. At the time, the poverty threshold for a family of four was an annual income of about $3,000.

Because so many Americans had not been shamed by *Harvest of Shame*, Chavez more than had his work cut out for him. In the face of attacks by hired thugs and jailings, through rallies, hunger strikes, labor strikes, Chavez and his colleagues raised awareness and brought pressure to bear on growers to raise the wages of people who tended their crops and to also provide them with better working and living conditions.

Chavez is best known as a co-organizer of a strike, combined with a call for a national boycott, against the growers of wine and table grapes of California's San Joaquin Valley. The crusade lasted for five years. It ended in 1970, with the UFW securing its first contract with grape growers.

Fourteen years later, at the Commonwealth Club of California, Chavez, dressed in simple pants, white shirt, and argyle vest, was still beating the drum for justice for agricultural workers. In his speech, Chavez reminded his wealthy audience dining on pork tenderloin that thousands of agricultural workers (called braceros, which is a Spanish word for migrant laborers) still lived and worked under wretched conditions.

As millions do today in America. And not all of them are agricultural workers.

BOYCOTT GRAPES

BOYCOTT GRAPES

Farm workers are not agricultural implements. They are not beasts of burden—to be used and discarded. . . .

TWENTY-ONE YEARS AGO LAST SEPTEMBER, ON A LONELY STRETCH OF RAILROAD TRACK PARALLELING US HIGHWAY 101 NEAR SALINAS, 32 BRACERO FARM WORKERS LOST THEIR LIVES IN A TRAGIC ACCIDENT.

The Braceros had been imported from Mexico to work on California farms. They died when their bus, which was converted from a flatbed truck, drove in front of a freight train.

Conversion of the bus had not been approved by any government agency. The driver had "tunnel" vision.

Most of the bodies lay unidentified for days. No one, including the grower who employed the workers, even knew their names.

Today, thousands of farm workers live under savage conditions—beneath trees and amid garbage and human excrement—near tomato fields in San Diego County, tomato fields which use the most modern farm technology.

Vicious rats gnaw on them as they sleep. They walk miles to buy food at inflated prices. And they carry in water from irrigation pumps.

Child labor is still common in many farm areas. . . .

Some 800,000 under-aged children work with their families harvesting crops across America. Babies born to migrant workers suffer 25 percent higher infant mortality than the rest of the population.

Malnutrition among migrant worker children is 10 times higher than the national rate.

Farm workers' average life expectancy is still 49 years—compared to 73 years for the average American.

All my life, I have been driven by one dream, one goal, one vision: To overthrow a farm labor system in this nation which treats farm workers as if they were not important human beings.

Farm workers are not agricultural implements. They are not beasts of burden—to be used and discarded. . . .

I began to realize what other minority people had discovered: That the only answer—the only hope—was in organizing. More of us had to become citizens. We had to register to vote. And people like me had to develop the skills it would take to organize, to educate, to help empower the Chicano people.

I spent many years—before we founded the union—learning how to work with people.

We experienced some successes in voter registration, in politics, in battling racial discrimination—successes in an era when Black Americans were just beginning to assert their civil rights and when political awareness among Hispanics was almost non-existent.

But deep in my heart, I knew I could never be happy unless I tried organizing the farm workers. I didn't know if I would succeed. But I had to try.

All Hispanics—urban and rural, young and old—are connected to the farm workers' experience. We had all lived through the fields—or our parents had. We shared that common humiliation.

How could we progress as a people, even if we lived in the cities, while the farm workers—men and women of our color—were condemned to a life without pride?

How could we progress as a people while the farm workers—who symbolized our history in this land—were denied self-respect?

How could our people believe that their children could become lawyers and doctors and judges and business people while this shame, this injustice was permitted to continue? . . .

The UFW was the beginning! We attacked that historical source of shame and infamy that our people in this country lived with. We attacked that injustice, not by complaining; not by seeking handouts; not by becoming soldiers in the War on Poverty.

We organized! . . .

Once social change begins, it cannot be reversed.

You cannot uneducate the person who has learned to read. You cannot humiliate the person who feels pride. You cannot oppress the people who are not afraid anymore.

Our opponents must understand that it's not just a union we have built. Unions, like other institutions, can come and go.

But we're more than an institution. For nearly 20 years, our union has been on the cutting edge of a people's cause— and you cannot do away with an entire people; you cannot stamp out a people's cause.

Regardless of what the future holds for the union, regardless of what the future holds for farm workers, our accomplishments cannot be undone. "La Causa"— our cause—doesn't have to be experienced twice.

The consciousness and pride that were raised by our union are alive and thriving inside millions of young Hispanics who will never work on a farm!

Like the other immigrant groups, the day will come when we win the economic and political rewards which are in keeping with our numbers in society. The day will come when the politicians do the right thing by our people out of political necessity and not out of charity or idealism.

That day may not come this year. That day may not come during this decade. But it will come, someday!

HILLARY RODHAM CLINTON

October 26, 1947–

REMARKS TO THE UN 4TH WORLD CONFERENCE
ON WOMEN, 1995

WOMEN'S
RIGHTS
ARE
HUMAN
RIGHTS

HILLARY RODHAM CLINTON

She was five years away from being elected to the US Senate (representing New York).

She was roughly thirteen years away from losing the Democratic party's presidential nomination to Barack Obama and, after he won the presidency, becoming his secretary of state.

And Hillary Diane Rodham Clinton was more than twenty years away from becoming her party's presidential candidate, then having her dream of being America's first female president dashed in a loss to Donald Trump.

Back on September 5, 1995, in the year that America celebrated the seventy-fifth anniversary of its women getting the national right to vote, Hillary Clinton, the tough, tenacious native of Chicago, was the first lady of the United States. And on that day, she spoke at the United Nations Fourth Conference on Women: Action for Equality, Development and Peace, held in Beijing, the capital of China. Hillary's husband, Bill, had won the presidency in 1992.

Some members of the Clinton administration did not want the First Lady to attend the conference. That was because it was held in

> We need to understand there is no one formula for how women should lead our lives.

China, a nation with an atrocious human rights record. But go she did. Once there, she did not hold her tongue.

When Hillary Clinton, forty-seven, addressed 17,000 delegates from 189 nations, she delivered a speech that packed a punch with its litany of the many and varied ways women and girls around the world are abused, mistreated, kept from the good things in life. Most memorably, Clinton declared that "human rights are women's rights, and women's rights are human rights."

That line, that moment, rocked the house. Clinton's then chief of staff, Melanne Verveer, who became the first US ambassador for global women's issues in 2009, remembered delegates with tears streaming down their faces, delegates stomping their feet.

Speaking in 2016 of Clinton's Beijing speech, Kathy Spillar, executive director of the Feminist Majority Foundation, said, "We look back 21 years later, and we go, 'duh'—but it was groundbreaking at the time. It was huge. . . . It was just an extraordinary moment in the centuries-long struggle for women's full human rights around the world."

"After the speech," reported Amy Chozick around the same time, "women dressed in traditional garb from various nations poured over an escalator to try to touch Mrs. Clinton, who wore a powder pink suit. Tens of thousands of workers with nongovernmental organizations [such as those involved in humanitarian aid and the campaign for human rights] who were not allowed to attend the conference, gathered amid a downpour and the heavy security in [Beijing] . . . to hear Mrs. Clinton deliver a version of the speech."

"Women's rights are human rights." Those five words from a twenty-one-minute speech became a manifesto for women around the globe. Those words fired up legions of women—and men—to fight on, fight on for gender justice, gender equality, a campaign that continues today.

The great challenge of this conference is to give voice to women everywhere. . . .

WOULD LIKE TO THANK THE SECRETARY GENERAL FOR INVITING ME TO BE PART OF THIS IMPORTANT UNITED NATIONS FOURTH WORLD CONFERENCE ON WOMEN. THIS IS TRULY A CELEBRATION, A CELEBRATION OF THE CONTRIBUTIONS WOMEN MAKE IN EVERY ASPECT OF LIFE: IN THE HOME, ON THE JOB, IN THE COMMUNITY, AS MOTHERS, WIVES, SISTERS, DAUGHTERS, LEARNERS, WORKERS, CITIZENS, AND LEADERS.

It is also a coming together, much the way women come together every day in every country. We come together in fields and factories, in village markets and supermarkets, in living rooms and board rooms. Whether it is while playing with our children in the park, or washing clothes in a river, or taking a break at the office water cooler, we come together and talk about our aspirations and concerns. And time and again, our talk turns to our children and our families. However different we may appear, there is far more that unites us than divides us. We share a common future, and we are here to find common ground so that we may help bring new dignity and respect to women and girls all over the world, and in so doing bring new strength and stability to families as well.

By gathering in Beijing, we are focusing world attention on issues that matter most in our lives—the lives of women

and their families: access to education, health care, jobs and credit, the chance to enjoy basic legal and human rights and to participate fully in the political life of our countries. . . .

What we are learning around the world is that if women are healthy and educated, their families will flourish. If women are free from violence, their families will flourish. If women have a chance to work and earn as full and equal partners in society, their families will flourish. And when families flourish, communities and nations do as well. That is why every woman, every man, every child, every family, and every nation on this planet does have a stake in the discussion that takes place here. . . .

The great challenge of this conference is to give voice to women everywhere whose experiences go unnoticed, whose words go unheard. Women comprise more than half the world's population, 70% of the world's poor, and two-thirds of those who are not taught to read and write. We are the primary caretakers for most of the world's children and elderly. Yet much of the work we do is not valued—not by economists, not by historians, not by popular culture, not by government leaders.

At this very moment, as we sit here, women around the world are giving birth, raising children, cooking meals, washing clothes, cleaning houses, planting crops, working on assembly lines, running companies, and running countries. Women also are dying from diseases that should have been prevented or treated. They are watching their children succumb to malnutrition caused by poverty and economic deprivation. They are being denied the right to go to school by their own fathers and brothers. They are being forced into prostitution, and they are being barred from the bank lending offices and banned from the ballot box.

Those of us who have the opportunity to be here have the responsibility to speak for those who could not. As an American, I want to speak for women in my own country, women who are raising children on the minimum wage, women who can't afford health care or child care, women whose lives are threatened by violence, including violence in their own homes. . . .

Speaking to you today, I speak for them, just as each of us speaks for women around the world who are denied the chance to go to school, or see a doctor, or own property, or have a say about the direction of their lives, simply because they are women. The truth is that most women around the world work both inside and outside the home, usually by necessity.

We need to understand there is no one formula for how women should lead our lives. That is why we must respect the choices that each woman makes for herself and her family. Every woman deserves the chance to realize her own God-given potential. But we must recognize that women will never gain full dignity until their human rights are respected and protected.

Our goals for this conference, to strengthen families and societies by empowering women to take greater control over their own destinies, cannot be fully achieved unless all governments—here and around the world—accept their responsibility to protect and promote internationally recognized human rights. The international community has long acknowledged and recently reaffirmed at Vienna that both women and men are entitled to a range of protections and personal freedoms, from the right of personal security to the right to determine freely the number and spacing of the children they bear. No one should be forced to remain silent for fear of religious or political persecution, arrest, abuse, or torture.

Tragically, women are most often the ones whose human rights are violated. Even now, in the late 20th century, the rape of women continues to be used as an instrument of armed conflict. Women and children make up a large majority of the world's refugees. And when women are excluded from the political process, they become even more vulnerable to abuse. I believe that now, on the eve of a new millennium, it is time to break the silence. It is time for us to say here in Beijing, and for the world to hear, that it is no longer acceptable to discuss women's rights as separate from human rights.

These abuses have continued because, for too long, the history of women has been a history of silence. Even today, there are those who are trying to silence our words. But the voices of this conference and of the women . . . must be heard loudly and clearly:

It is a violation of human rights when babies are denied food, or drowned, or suffocated, or their spines broken, simply because they are born girls.

It is a violation of human rights when women and girls are sold into the slavery of prostitution for human greed—and the kinds of reasons that are used to justify this practice should no longer be tolerated.

It is a violation of human rights when women are doused with gasoline, set on fire, and burned to death because their marriage dowries are deemed too small.

It is a violation of human rights when individual women are raped in their own communities and when thousands of women are subjected to rape as a tactic or prize of war.

It is a violation of human rights when a leading cause of death worldwide among women ages 14 to 44 is the violence they are subjected to in their own homes by their own relatives.

. . .

It is a violation of human rights when women are denied the right to plan their own families, and that includes being forced to have abortions or being sterilized against their will.

If there is one message that echoes forth from this conference, let it be that human rights are women's rights and women's rights are human rights once and for all. Let us not forget that among those rights are the right to speak freely—and the right to be heard.

Women must enjoy the rights to participate fully in the social and political lives of their countries, if we want freedom and democracy to thrive and endure. It is indefensible that many women in nongovernmental organizations who wished to participate in this conference have not been able to attend—or have been prohibited from fully taking part.

Let me be clear. Freedom means the right of people to assemble, organize, and debate openly. It means respecting the views of those who may disagree with the views of their governments. It means not taking citizens away from their loved ones and jailing them, mistreating them, or denying them their freedom or dignity because of the peaceful expression of their ideas and opinions.

In my country, we recently celebrated

the 75th anniversary of Women's Suffrage. It took 150 years after the signing of our Declaration of Independence for women to win the right to vote. It took 72 years of organized struggle, before that happened, on the part of many courageous women and men. It was one of America's most divisive philosophical wars. But it was a bloodless war. Suffrage was achieved without a shot being fired.

But we have also been reminded, in V-J Day observances last weekend, of the good that comes when men and women join together to combat the forces of tyranny and to build a better world. We have seen peace prevail in most places for a half century. We have avoided another world war. But we have not solved older, deeply rooted problems that continue to diminish the potential of half the world's population.

Now it is the time to act on behalf of women everywhere. If we take bold steps to better the lives of women, we will be taking bold steps to better the lives of children and families too. Families rely on mothers and wives for emotional support and care. Families rely on women for labor in the home. And increasingly, everywhere, families rely on women for income needed to raise healthy children and care for other relatives.

As long as discrimination and inequities remain so commonplace everywhere in the world, as long as girls and women are valued less, fed less, fed last, overworked, underpaid, not schooled, subjected to violence in and outside their homes—the potential of the human family to create a peaceful, prosperous world will not be realized.

Let this conference be our—and the world's—call to action. Let us heed that call so we can create a world in which every woman is treated with respect and dignity, every boy and girl is loved and cared for equally, and every family has the hope of a strong and stable future. That is the work before you. That is the work before all of us who have a vision of the world we want to see—for our children and our grandchildren.

The time is now. We must move beyond rhetoric. We must move beyond recognition of problems to working together, to have the common efforts to build that common ground we hope to see.

God's blessings on you, your work, and all who will benefit from it.

Godspeed and thank you very much.

NOTE FROM TONYA BOLDEN

While working on the introductions to the eloquence collected herein, over and again I thought, *So much is possible!*

An enslaved boy rising to revered national leader . . . a former president and member of a prominent family seeing and saluting the value of everyday men and women . . . a slugger bearing up under great pain . . . a sharecropper daring to question her country on a national stage . . .

And a fledging nation did indeed endure.

In bearing witness to American possibilities, these speeches also inspire us, rally us, call us to think, to search our hearts and minds for ways we can join forces with those seeking to right wrongs that still plague American society, that hold the nation back from truly being its best self, a place of more dynamic possibilities, of broader opportunities, of true liberty, of true justice for all people, regardless of . . .

Everything.

For these strong voices also remind us, in ways subtle and bold, of our common humanity.

NOTE FROM ERIC VELASQUEZ

Working on *Strong Voices* has been a transformative experience. As an illustrator, my job is to read through the manuscript several times in order to get a good idea of what the visuals should be. However, with this project the more I researched each speech, looking at reference photographs and then creating a storyboard, and the more I read through the magnificent speeches delivered by these exceptional Americans during different periods in American history, the more I realized how much I identified with each one of the speeches. I was already familiar with most of the speeches, except for those by Red Jacket and Langston Hughes. Nevertheless I felt a sense of familiarity with all the voices present in this collection. Suddenly, I had the realization that I am an American illustrator with the task of illustrating the voices of my country. As an African American (and the son of immigrants) in America, I don't always feel welcomed in all the spaces I enter, yet here among these voices are the elements of what binds us together as Americans: the shared dreams, aspirations, future expectations, and fears of my country. The speeches resonated and inspired me to think of what America could ultimately become.

Eric Vel

DECEMBER 16, 1773: *The Boston Tea Party*

MARCH 23, 1775: *Give Me Liberty or Give Me Death!*
PATRICK HENRY

1805: *We Never Quarrel about Religion*
RED JACKET

JULY 4, 1776: The Declaration of Independence is signed

War of 1812
1812–1815

Revolutionary War
1775–1783

APRIL 30, 1789:
George Washington is inaugurated

SEPTEMBER 19, 1796: George Washington's Farewell Address is published
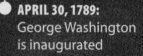
GEORGE WASHINGTON

SEPTEMBER 3, 1783: The Treaty of Paris is signed, ending the American Revolution

May 7, 1957: *On the Blacklist All Our Lives*
LANGSTON HUGHES

July 4, 1939:
Farewell to Baseball
LOU GEHRIG

Vietnam War
1955–1975

Korean War **1950–1953**

World War II
1939–1945

October 4, 1957: The Soviet Union launches Sputnik, the first artificial satellite, starting the Space Race

January 20, 1961:
John F. Kennedy is inaugurated

September 12, 1962:
We Choose to Go to the Moon
JOHN F. KENNEDY

1964: The Civil Rights Act of 1964 passes, a landmark civil rights and labor law outlawing discrimination based on race, color, religion, sex, or national origin

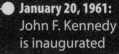

August 1962: Fannie Lou Hamer and colleagues attempt to register to vote, are attacked and imprisoned

August 28, 1963: *I Have a Dream*
MARTIN LUTHER KING JR.

August 22, 1964: Fannie Lou testifies before the Credentials Committee at the Democratic National Convention
FANNIE LOU HAMER

May 29, 1851: *I Am a Woman's Rights*
SOJOURNER TRUTH

April 23, 1863: The *New York Independent* publishes the Frances Dana Gage verison of Sojourner Truth's speech

March 4, 1861: Abraham Lincoln is inaugurated

November 19, 1863: The Gettysburg Address
ABRAHAM LINCOLN

1870: The Fifteenth Amendment gives black men the national vote

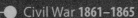

Civil War 1861–1865

1865: The Thirteenth Amendment abolishes slavery

July 5, 1852: *What to the Slave Is the Fourth of July?*
FREDERICK DOUGLASS

1896–1965: Jim Crow laws, which make racial discrimination legal, are in effect

The Great Depression **1929–1939**

1920: The Nineteenth Amendment gives women the national vote

World War I **1914–1918**

September 14, 1901: Theodore Roosevelt is inaugurated

October 24, 1929: The stock market crashes, starting the Great Depression

April 23, 1910: Citizenship in a Republic, commonly known as "The Man in the Arena"
THEODORE ROOSEVELT

March 4, 1933: *The Only Thing We Have to Fear Is Fear Itself*
FRANKLIN DELANO ROOSEVELT

TIMELINE

November 9, 1984: Cesar Chavez gives address to the Commonwealth Club of California
CESAR CHAVEZ

1965-1970: The Delano Grape Strike and Boycott, organized by Cesar Chavez

July 20, 1969: Neil Armstrong sets foot on the moon

Gulf War **1990–1991**

September 5, 1995: *Women's Rights Are Human Rights*
HILLARY RODHAM CLINTON

NOTES AND SOURCES

PATRICK HENRY

"unearthly fire . . . whipcords": Harlow Giles Unger, *Lion of Liberty: Patrick Henry and the Call to a New Nation* (Cambridge, MA: Da Capo Press, 2010), p. 97.

GEORGE WASHINGTON

"'every attempt to alienate . . . that make us one": "Read the Full Transcript of President Obama's Farewell Speech," *Los Angeles Times*, January 10, 2017, www.latimes.com/politics/la-pol-obama -farewell-speech-transcript-20170110-story.html.

RED JACKET

"There is but one . . . darkness": Granville Ganter, ed. "Reply to Rev. Jacob Cram," *The Collected Speeches of Sagoyewatha, or Red Jacket* (Syracuse, NY: Syracuse University Press, 2006), pp. 139–140.

FREDERICK DOUGLASS

"twin-monsters of darkness": Frederick Douglass, "The Folly of Our Opponents," in Philip S. Foner and Yuval Taylor, eds., *Frederick Douglass: Selected Speeches and Writings* (Chicago: Lawrence Hill Books, 1999), Kindle edition.

"all men are . . . Happiness": Declaration of Independence, Our Documents, www.ourdocuments.gov/doc.php?flash =false&doc=2&page=transcript.

SOJOURNER TRUTH

"Strange compound of wit and wisdom . . . common sense": Nell Irvin Painter, *Sojourner Truth: A Life, A Symbol* (New York: W. W. Norton, 1996), p. 98.

"A woman of remarkable . . . beautifully powerful": Nell Irvin Painter, ibid., p. 3.

"Well, chillen, whar dar's . . . kilter": "Compare the Two Speeches," www.thesojournertruthproject .com/compare-the-speeches.

"It is impossible to transfer it . . . strong and truthful tones": Marius R. Robinson, "Women's Rights Convention," *Anti-Slavery Bugle*, June 21, 1851, p. 160.

ABRAHAM LINCOLN

"A GLORIOUS VICTORY!" *Boston Daily Advertiser*, July 6, 1863, p. 1.

"a few appropriate remarks": https://www .loc.gov/exhibits/gettysburg-address/ext /trans-formal.html.

"sallow, sunken-eyed . . . quiet": Henry Clay Cochrane, "With Lincoln to Gettysburg, 1863," (Gettys-burg) *Star & Sentinel*, May 22, 1907, p. 1.

"Standing beneath this serene sky . . . THE BATTLES OF GETTYSBURG": www.voicesofdemocracy.umd.edu/everett -gettysburg-address-speech-text.

"the crown jewel of American rhetoric": Hal Gordon, "The Gettysburg Address: America's Greatest Speech," The Commentator, November 21, 2013, www.thecommentator.com/article/4379 /the_gettysburg_address_america_s _greatest_speech.

LOU GEHRIG

"without doubt one . . . swallow hard": John Drebinger, "61,808 Fans Roar Tribute to Gehrig," *New York Times*, July 5, 1939, p. 21.

"The clangy, iron echo of the . . . luckiest man . . .": Steve Wulf, "An Awful Lot to Live for," ESPN.com, July 4, 2014, www.espn.com/mlb/story/_/id/11159148/mlb-lou-gehrig-farewell-speech-75-years-later.

"We love you, Lou!": "The Day Lou Gehrig Made Yankee Stadium Weep," *New York Times*, June 2, 2016, www.nytimes.com/interactive/projects/cp/obituaries/archives/lou-gehrig-yankee-stadium.

JOHN FITZGERALD KENNEDY

"Apollo riding his chariot . . . program": Emily Kennard, "What's in a Name?" www.nasa.gov/centers/glenn/about/history/silverstein_feature.html.

"one small step . . . one giant leap": Tonya Bolden, *Pathfinders: The Journeys of 16 Extraordinary Black Souls* (New York: Abrams, 2017), p. 106.

MARTIN LUTHER KING JR.

"Tell them about . . . the dream!" Tonya Bolden, *M.L.K.: The Journey of a King* (New York: Abrams, 2006), p. 80.

"The end is reconciliation . . .": Tonya Bolden, ibid., p. 36.

CESAR CHAVEZ

"The dark brown man's deep sad eyes . . . face of Cesar Chavez": Miriam Pawel, *The Crusades of Cesar Chavez: A Biography* (New York: Bloomsbury, 2014), p. 1.

On the poverty threshold: "Weighted Average Poverty Thresholds for Families, 1960–2012," https://www.infoplease.com/business-finance/poverty-and-income/weighted-average-poverty-thresholds1-families-1960-2012.

HILLARY RODHAM CLINTON

"We look back 21 years later . . . around the world": Jocelyn Noveck, "Why a 1995 Speech Proved Formative for Clinton," August 20, 2016, PBS Newshour, www.pbs.org/newshour/politics/1995-speech-china-clinton.

"After the speech . . . of the speech": Amy Chozick, "Hillary Clinton's Beijing Speech on Women Resonates 20 Years Later," September 5, 2015, *New York Times*, www.nytimes.com/politics/first-draft/2015/09/05/20-years-later-hillary-clintons-beijing-speech-on-women-resonates.

PERMISSIONS